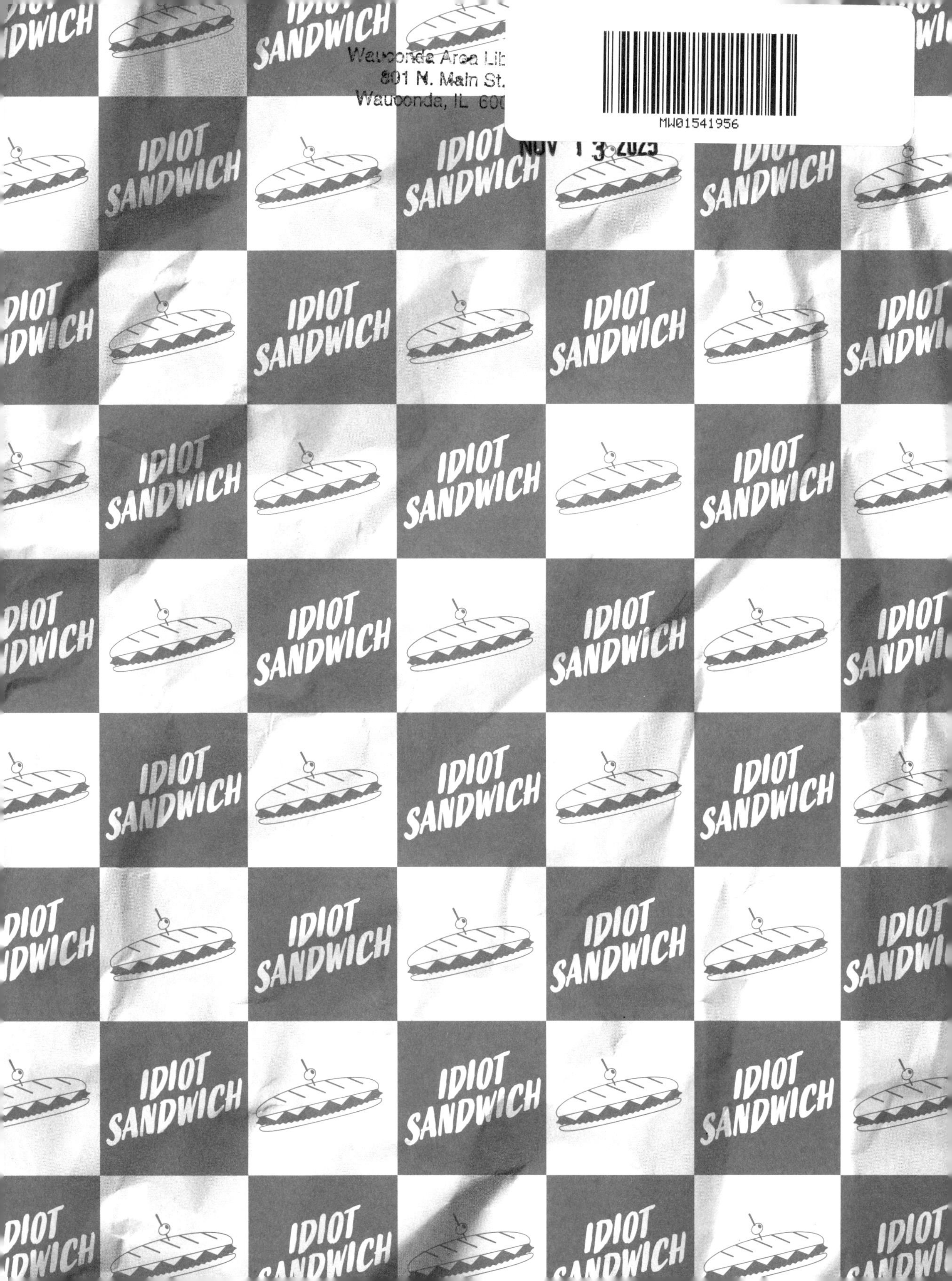
IDIOT SANDWICH

IDIOT SANDWICH

IDIOT SANDWICH

100+ Recipes to Elevate Your Sandwich Game

Without limiting the exclusive rights of any author, contributor or the publisher of this publication, any unauthorized use of this publication to train generative artificial intelligence (AI) technologies is expressly prohibited. HarperCollins also exercise their rights under Article 4(3) of the Digital Single Market Directive 2019/790 and expressly reserve this publication from the text and data mining exception.

IDIOT SANDWICH. Copyright © 2025 by Studio Ramsay Global LLC. All rights reserved. Printed in Canada. No part of this book may be used or reproduced in any manner whatsoever without written permission except in the case of brief quotations embodied in critical articles and reviews. For information, address HarperCollins Publishers, 195 Broadway, New York, NY 10007. In Europe, HarperCollins Publishers, Macken House, 39/40 Mayor Street Upper, Dublin 1, D01 C9W8, Ireland.

HarperCollins books may be purchased for educational, business, or sales promotional use. For information, please email the Special Markets Department at SPsales@harpercollins.com.

hc.com

FIRST EDITION

Foreword: Gordon Ramsay
Author: Courtney McBroom
Photographer: Lindsay Kreighbaum
Illustrator: Faye Orlove
Culinary Supervisor and Recipe Author: Avery Pursell
Recipe Developers: Codii Lopez, Kesha Tatro
Recipe Testers: Chelsey Bawot, Joey Firoben, Veronica Laramie,
   Aubrey Neuman, Zoe Roemer, Gary Walker
Production Supervisor: Elle Rose
Prop Stylist: Aimie Vredevoogd
Food Stylist: Veronica Laramie
Food Stylist Assistants: Diana Kim, Vanessa Santana, Daniela Swamp
Production Assistant: Leslie "Texas" Turner

Cover Photographer: Brian Bowen Smith
Image courtesy of *Sandwich Magazine*, the Chef's Special Issue
Designed by Nancy Singer

Library of Congress Cataloging-in-Publication Data has been applied for.

ISBN 978-0-06-343672-5

25 26 27 28 29 TC 10 9 8 7 6 5 4 3 2 1

"IN ORDER TO REACH PERFECTION, ONE MUST BEGIN BY BEING IGNORANT OF A GREAT DEAL."

—FYODOR DOSTOEVSKY, *THE IDIOT*

CONTENTS

FOREWORD	viii
INTRODUCTION	x
WHAT EVERY IDIOT NEEDS TO KNOW	xv
MORNING	xxviii
NOON	52
NIGHT	104
SWEET	160
CONDIMENTS	192
INDEX	217

FOREWORD

It's truly unbelievable we're here!

Who knew that two slices of bread would turn into a global phenom when I first did that now infamous short sketch on late-night television years ago. I had no idea it would go on to create a mega meme, an amazing digital series, and this fantastic cookbook. All celebrating the thing anyone can do at home: make a sandwich.

Everywhere I go, people ask me to turn them into an "Idiot Sandwich"—first it was autographs, then selfies, now it's this. My daughters' friends asked me to do it when I did the school run, when I'm queuing for coffee or even out on my bike . . . it's everywhere. But I love turning people into "Idiot Sandwiches" and it's incredible how many people it's reached—I think we all need to be reminded we are an idiot sandwich once in a while.

Over the years I've been in some of the best kitchens in the world, using the finest ingredients out there. But as a chef, I know there's nothing—and I mean *nothing*—that tastes better than a sandwich you make yourself after service.

Chefs, of course, are the best sandwich makers on the planet—but we're lucky because we've got the opportunity to experiment with the most incredible meats, fresh veg, salads, fruits, preparation techniques, breads, and condiments you can only dream about. I remember finishing service one night at Claridge's in London and we'd saved all the Beef Wellington ends for our staff dinner. A light bulb went off in my head and I thought, "I'm going to make a Beef Wellington sandwich!" So, I slapped them between two slices of sourdough, slathered on some truffle mayonnaise, and banged it together. I was as happy as the proverbial pig in you know what. To me, the secret of what makes a great sandwich is wanting to eat it all over again the minute you've finished.

Social media has truly let people run wild to conjure up incredible flavour combinations and creations. I really think I've seen it all based on all the weird stuff people send me on social media. I've reacted to countless sandwich videos in my "Ramsay Reacts" series, but one really stood out to me a few months back. It was about a foot in height and there was something like 490 slices of cheese with ham in it (I slowed it down about a hundred times to count). This thing was sandwiched together, floured, egg washed, breadcrumbed, and deep fried. It was totally amazing!

That's what the *Idiot Sandwich* book is really about—celebrating the best sandwiches from different places, cultures, and walks of life, and the way that, at some point, someone stopped and thought: "What if I change it up a bit . . . ?" It takes an idiot (and I mean it as a term of endearment) to imagine and create the most exciting and inspiring sandwiches on the planet. Every day someone, somewhere is inventing a new sandwich. And trust me, I'm one of them.

So, I hope you enjoy and can be your own Idiot Sandwich with this book.

INTRODUCTION

"WHAT ARE YOU?!?"
"An idiot sandwich."
"IDIOT SANDWICH WHAT?!"
"An idiot sandwich, Chef Ramsay!"

Hey there. Welcome to our little book about sandwiches. It's good of you to drop by. Can we offer you a beer? Oh, perhaps something with a little more pep, then. Here, have an iced coffee. Go ahead, take a seat and make yourself at home. You're probably wondering how we got here. Well, it's all because of a heated exchange in a comedy sketch; the one you just read, right up there at the top of this page. Unless you've been living under a rock, you must have heard of the idiot sandwich meme. That's when those words were first uttered. You know, the one where Gordon Ramsay holds two pieces of bread on either side of a famous TV host's face, and she calls herself an idiot sandwich. The concept went viral immediately first as a YouTube video, then as a meme, then as a show, and now, with any luck, this book. By the way, on the off chance you *have* been living under a rock, don't worry, we get it. Housing is unreasonably expensive these days.

It's not exactly a savvy business move to call people idiots. One could even argue that it would deter them from reading this cookbook. We have a great reason, though, and we'd like to tell you, if you'll let us. So, pull your chair a little closer to the fire while we add another ice cube to your coffee. It's time to settle in for a segment we like to call: "Idiot Sandwich and You."

According to *Merriam-Webster*, the term *idiot* means "a foolish or stupid person," but its root can be traced all the way back to the Greek word *idio*, which means "distinct." *Idiosyncrasy* and *idiom* have the same root, and both of those words relate to "distinctness" in one way or another. We tell you this because we should all be so lucky to be called an idiot. And not in the way *Merriam-Webster* defines it. In the way the Greeks do, with the root of the word itself—*idio*.

Here's the thing. We aren't calling you an idiot to demean you. We would never do that. We're giving you *permission* to be one. Wear the label with pride. Be distinct. Stand strong in your ignorance. None of us understands everything there is to know in the world, especially when it comes to sandwiches. We'd be foolish to say we did. (Just to be clear, though, we do know A LOT about sandwiches. We have Gordon Ramsay in our court, and we've spent the better part of a year creating these recipes and testing them to perfection.) The only way to become less foolish is to do the thing anyway, even if you have no idea what you are doing. Cooking is trial and error. It's about the journey, not the destination, even though the destination is almost always delicious. Focus on having fun and sharing sandwiches with the people you love. Embrace not needing to be the smartest person in the room. The world needs more people who are curious; people who can admit they don't know all the answers. This may seem counterintuitive, but the only way to overcome the problem of idiocy is to act like a complete and utter idiot.

The good news is, if you use this book correctly, you'll go from idiot to idiot savant in no time. The better news is there's no wrong way to use this book. There are a few things you should know going into it, though. More on that on the next page. But if you ever start to feel nervous or like it's all too much, remember this: We aren't performing brain surgery. Any idiot can make a sandwich.

A Brief History OF THE Sandwich

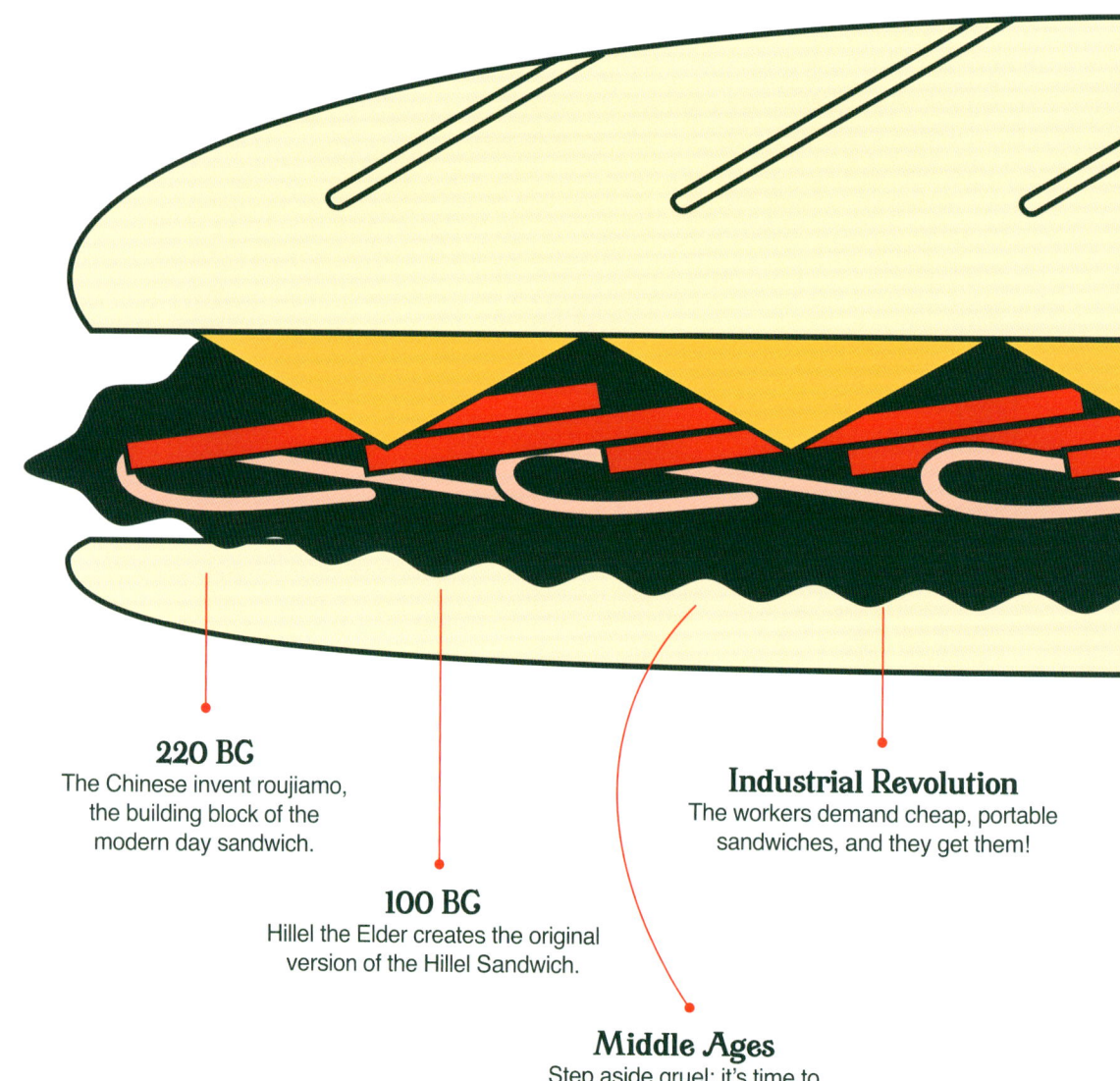

220 BC
The Chinese invent roujiamo, the building block of the modern day sandwich.

100 BC
Hillel the Elder creates the original version of the Hillel Sandwich.

Middle Ages
Step aside gruel; it's time to welcome trenchers to the table.

Industrial Revolution
The workers demand cheap, portable sandwiches, and they get them!

1832
Mrs. N. K. M. Lee publishes the first sandwich recipe and, completely unrelated, the first kosher deli opens in New York City.

1926
Otto Rohwedder invents the first bread slicing machine and Gustav Papendick creates a way to package the new loaves in what would become the greatest invention since sliced bread

1930
Wonder Bread hits shelves nationwide.

Present
Americans eat over 300 million sandwiches a day.

Future
New civilizations dawn and among them, new sandwiches are born.

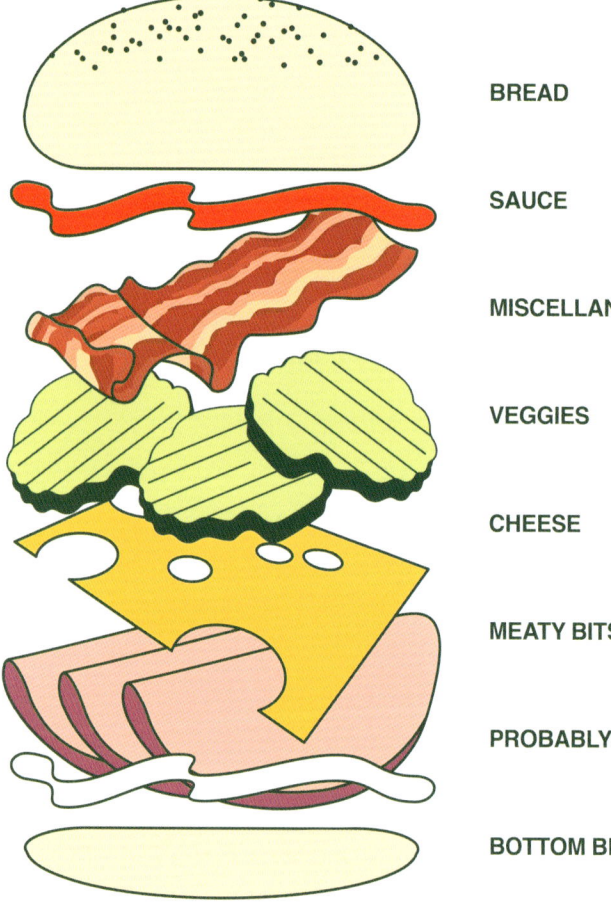

WHAT EVERY IDIOT NEEDS TO KNOW

In a perfect world, we'd eat sandwiches for every meal. And since we can create any world we want with this book, we've done just that. It's divvied up into three sections based on time of day—morning, noon, and night—so you can have a sandwich whenever you want. We also include a bonus *Sweet* chapter for those who prefer their sandwiches with a little sugar on top. Most importantly, we've added a separate chapter just for the condiments. There you'll find over thirty recipes for all of the tasty sauces, pickles, and crunchy bits that we use throughout the book. (It's the condiments that make the sandwich, after all.)

As for the sandwiches themselves, OF COURSE we are going to provide recipes for every little aspect of them, but while we believe that homemade is best, we know everyone is busy and tired. It's important to make these sandwiches in a way that's approachable to you, so if that means supporting your local doughboy instead of making biscuits from scratch, then we are all for it. To each idiot their own. With that in mind, we'll offer plenty of options for items that can be purchased premade to save time and energy. You can read more about those in our pantry, bread, and condiment sections, as well as in the recipes themselves.

Before we leave you to your own devices, one more word of advice. Tee yourself up by getting all of your mise en place prepped and ready ahead of time. For those who don't speak kitchenese, *mise en place* is the term for setting up all of the tools and ingredients necessary for the creation of your recipe. It will make the assembly go all that more quickly so you can spend less time in the kitchen and more time on the thing that really matters—eating sandwiches.

PANTRY

Butter: We're gonna tell you to toast a lot of bread in a lot of butter in this book. We prefer unsalted butter, then season to taste, but you can use salted if that's all you have. Simply adjust the seasoning as necessary.

Herbs and spices: You'll need both fresh and dried herbs for various recipes here. We'll be sure to tell you which to use in the ingredient list. Dried are typically stronger than fresh, so if you need to sub for either, use half the amount of dried, or double the amount of fresh. Dried herbs and spices are best kept in a cool, dry place. They will lose potency after a year or so, so best to replace any that have collected a good amount of dust.

Oils: Canola, grapeseed, and vegetable oil will work for frying or anytime a neutral oil is called for. They are called neutral oils because they don't impart any flavor. Extra-virgin olive oil, on the other hand, does impart flavor. It also has a lower smoke point, so it's not a great choice for frying. It is, however, great for things like sauteing at lower temperatures, salad dressings, and drizzling to finish a dish.

Salts: All salt references are for kosher salt. We tested our recipes specifically with Diamond Crystal brand. If you are using Morton's, it will be stronger, so start with a little less and adjust to taste.

Sour items: Sour, acidic ingredients like pickles, cornichons, capers, or even mustard are an important addition to every sandwich maker's arsenal. They help balance flavors and cut richness. Make sure your cupboards are stocked.

Spicy items: We love to bring the heat with dried chiles, harissa paste, gochujang, chipotle chiles, and all of the hot sauces that exist under the sun. If you don't like spicy things, these are ingredients you can cut back on or omit—just don't tell us you did.

Stocks and broths: If you have extra meat, bones, or vegetable peels lying around, it's best to make these at home, but beef, chicken, and vegetable stocks and broths can also be purchased from the grocery store. Stocks are made from bones; they have more collagen and a richer flavor. Broths are typically made from meat; they have a stronger, meatier flavor and are great for braising and sauces. In either case, go for reduced-sodium varieties to gain more control over the seasoning.

Sweet items: Sweet ingredients like brown sugar, honey, and maple syrup help balance the salty profiles in many of our sandwiches, and they are essential in the Sweet Treats chapter. Unless you have a major dietary concern, don't omit them.

Umami items: We use ingredients like chicken bouillon, fish sauce, miso, and Worcestershire sauce to lend depth and savoriness to our recipes. If you see them in the ingredient list, don't skip them. Generally speaking, these items have a long shelf life, so there's no reason not to keep them around.

Vinegars: You'll find balsamic, cider, malt, red wine, white wine, and rice vinegar in this book. If you can, use the type we call for, but if you don't want to make a trip to the grocery store, they are all interchangeable—just be aware that the flavor will change depending on which type of vinegar you use. The darker vinegars are deeper and earthier, while the lighter ones tend to be more flowery and crisp.

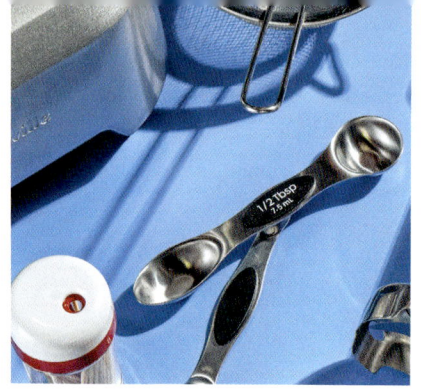
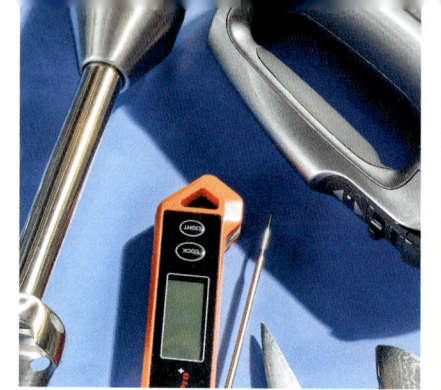

EQUIPMENT

KNIVES

Chef's knife: You'll need one of these, and it should be sharp. Get a stone and a honing steel and watch some YouTube instructional videos to help. It's really easy to keep a sharp knife, and it makes a world of difference in ease and technique.

Serrated knife: This is a must-have, as it is best for cutting bread and there is no substitute.

POTS AND PANS

Cast-iron skillet: A classic kitchen essential. It cooks evenly and can also double as weight if you need to make a pressed sandwich without a panini maker.

Grill pan: If you don't mind whether there are grill marks on your sandwich, you can use any other pan instead. It will taste the same, it just won't look as fancy. A grill pan is a great investment, though. Look for one that flips over as a griddle on the other side for optimal versatility.

Nonstick pans: These are great to cook eggs in and they make cleanup a breeze.

Sauce pots: Use these to make sauces (obviously) or for anything that requires cooking in a higher-volume receptacle.

SMALL APPLIANCES

Blenders and processors: In a perfect world, you'd have an immersion blender, a food processor, and a high-speed blender. Since this is not a perfect world, you can get by with just one, and it should be the high-speed blender.

Stand mixer: If you don't have one, use hand beaters. And if you don't have those, use a wooden spoon or a whisk. Skip arm day at the gym afterward.

Countertop fryer: Substitute by filling a large stockpot halfway with oil. Use a thermometer to keep track of the temperature, adjusting the heat as necessary.

Panini press: This is convenient for pressed sandwiches, but if you don't have one, heat the sandwich in a pan on the stovetop, cover the top with a small piece of parchment, and use a heavy offset spatula or a light weight to press down on it as it cooks.

BASICS

Box grater
Cooling rack
Liquid measuring cups
Measuring cups and spoons
Mixing bowls
Parchment paper
Potato masher
Rolling pin
Rubber spatula
Sheet tray
Tongs
Vegetable peeler
Whisk
Wooden spoon

NOT SO BASICS

Fish spatula: A regular spatula works, but a fish spatula is tops for when you need an ultra-thin, flexible flipping apparatus.

Mandolin: Use with caution, as they can be hazardous. A julienne tool, box grater, or simple knife cuts are great substitutions, but the mandoline is almost always faster.

Mason jars: Use these to store all those condiments you are about to make (page 192).

Microplane: A thin metal tool with a serrated edge, used to finely grate things like citrus, garlic, and hard cheeses.

Parchment paper: Great for easy cleanups and helps prevent burning or over darkening food.

Ring cutter: Use an upside-down drinking glass in a pinch.

Spider: Most often used to strain food from fry oil or boiling water. A slotted spoon or tongs will also do the trick.

Thermometer: Grab a high-temperature instant-read or candy thermometer for things like temping fry oil and meat, and an oven thermometer to make sure your oven stays the correct temperature.

Zip-top bag: These aren't just for carrying your favorite sandwiches. They're also perfect for marinating meats and storing leftovers, without the bulk of traditional food containers.

BREADS

Bread is arguably the most important part of a sandwich, and it needs to match the filling for best results. Don't throw a bunch of sauced-up meatballs on a thin piece of white sandwich bread—it'll be a mess. And don't layer a thick piece of ciabatta with a thin slice of deli meat. You'll tear the roof of your mouth to bits.

Bagels: Bagels are boiled in alkaline water before baking, giving them a dense, chewy texture. There are tons of flavors to choose from, all of which are delicious, so choose your best fighter and go from there.

Baguette: It doesn't get more French, or more classic, than a baguette. Long, thin, with a thick, crispy crust—it'll look so cute poking out of your tote bag next to a bouquet of flowers as you bike along the boulevard. Best used with heartier fillings, or some really great cheese. Sub with a crusty Italian loaf or ciabatta.

Biscuits: The American biscuit is a fluffy, flaky, and buttery quick bread that's a staple of Southern cuisine. They are best made from scratch, but if you are short on time, you can buy the dough from the store—unless you are in England, because there "biscuit" is actually the term for an American cookie, and what a hilarious misunderstanding *that* would be.

Buns: These come in many varieties, and they are generally interchangeable. The classic hamburger bun is the most recognizable, with white, wheat, potato, and brioche versions. There's also the Austrian kaiser roll, which can be topped with sesame seeds, poppy seeds, onion, or a simple sprinkle of salt. Telera are slightly sweet and round rolls that hail from Mexico and Central America. They are often used for tortas.

Brioche: A soft, rich, and buttery bread that's slightly sweet and almost cake-like. (Marie Antoi-

nette thought so, anyway.) Brioche is available in many forms, including a long roll that's often used for lobster. Challah and plain white bread are fine substitutes.

Challah: A traditional Jewish braided loaf that's soft, slightly sweet, and occasionally has additional mix-ins like raisins. Brioche can be used as a substitute.

Ciabatta: This famous Italian bread wasn't created until 1982. Its airy insides and extra crispy crust make it a perfect contender for heavy, saucy fillings. It comes as a large loaf, an individual roll, and every size in between, making it one of the more versatile breads in any sandwich maker's arsenal. An Italian loaf or focaccia can be substituted in a pinch.

Croissants: Not to be confused with the croissant *loaf* (see below), these buttery, flaky numbers come in all sizes. Choose what's best for you.

Croissant loaf: Once upon a time, a total genius took a croissant and turned it into a loaf of bread. It's light and buttery, just like a typical croissant, and can be found in most grocery stores or specialty bakeries. If you have trouble sourcing it, brioche or a plain white loaf will do the trick.

Cuban bread: A soft white baguette-shaped loaf that is quite similar to an Italian or French loaf, which coincidentally also make great substitutions for it. These can be found in most Latin markets.

English muffin bread: This is an English muffin, but in loaf form. They can be found in most grocery stores, but if you can't find one, substitute with plain white bread or sourdough.

Focaccia: A thick Italian flatbread recognizable by the dimples on top, it's slathered with oil before baking and often topped with herbs or other aromatics. Substitute with ciabatta rolls, if needed.

Hoagies: Hoagies, subs, grinders, and heroes are different names for the same thing—long, soft, individual rolls with a crust. They can be cut all the way through, or left hinged to help keep the fillings inside, making them great for heartier, saucier sandwiches. Italian and French rolls are most often used, but bolillo rolls and small Cuban and

Vietnamese loaves fall into this category as well. The softer-crusted varieties are great for crab rolls and classic deli meat sandos.

Milk bread: A pillowy white bread from Japan, it's similar to the Pullman loaf, except it doesn't use eggs and it's made with milk instead of water, hence the name. Loaves can be found in most Asian grocery stores. Swap with Hawaiian bread or plain white bread in a pinch.

Naan: Naan is a fluffy, yeasted flatbread used most often in Southern Asian cuisine and cooked in a tandoor oven. Other flatbreads like pita, roti, or lavash make great substitutions.

Pita: Pita is a round flatbread that originated in the Middle East. It puffs as it bakes, creating a large pocket that's perfect for stuffing.

Pretzel bread: Just like pretzels (and bagels), these loaves are boiled in alkaline water before baking, giving them that signature chewy crust and soft fluffy inside. They come as buns as well, and while not an exact swap, you can use brioche in a pinch.

Rye: A loaf of rye can come in many forms. Dark rye utilizes all three layers of the rye berry and has a darker, more intense flavor than light rye, which is mostly made of the endosperm. Light rye can have additions like dill and caraway to give it more flavor, and marbled rye is a swirled combination of both light and dark. Pumpernickel is a whole new beast. It's the hardest and densest of all because it's made from coarsely ground berries. Substitute a sourdough, country white, or wheat loaf, if needed.

Sourdough: Made with fermented dough, this loaf is slightly tangy and chewy with a crispy, crunchy crust. It is easy to find, but you can substitute with plain white bread.

Sprouted wheat: Sprouted wheat is made from ground wheat kernels that have been allowed to germinate, making it extra healthy and easier to digest. It can be swapped with regular wheat or plain white bread.

White bread: This is the classic white sandwich bread we all know and love, also known as a Pullman loaf. It's square, it's soft, and it's a great base to build flavor on. You can swap this with whole wheat or sprouted wheat if you want. If you are substituting this style of bread for any other type of loaf in this book, opt for a loaf that is sliced as thickly as possible.

NOTES FOR THE IDIOTS

To keep bread fresh, store it in a cool, dry place in a semi-breathable container like a paper bag, bread box, or wax paper. The freezer works, too, but you risk sogginess if any ice crystals develop. And don't forget, a serrated knife is always the best tool for slicing a loaf, so get one and love it.

GETTING TOASTY

There are about as many ways to toast a slice of bread as there are to make a sandwich, which is to say . . . lots. Toasters are the obvious choice, but you can't slather the bread in delicious butter first when you use them, so we prefer to toast our bread in an oven, under a broiler, or in a pan on the stovetop. You could even hold it over a bonfire. Just remember that the higher the temperature and the closer the bread is to the heat source, the faster it will toast. Play around with your levels. The darker the toast, the more flavorful it will be, up to a point. If you burn it, it will taste quite bitter, or as Gordon might say, "like your grandpa's old boot," but some people prefer that taste, so you do you. True connoisseurs will tell you to slather your bread with mayonnaise or butter before toasting it. And they are correct. Mayo lends a more neutral flavor, and it browns more evenly. Butter is richer and creamier. You could also toast it in a flavored oil, compound butter, or cheese, like we do with the Sky High Reuben (page 66).

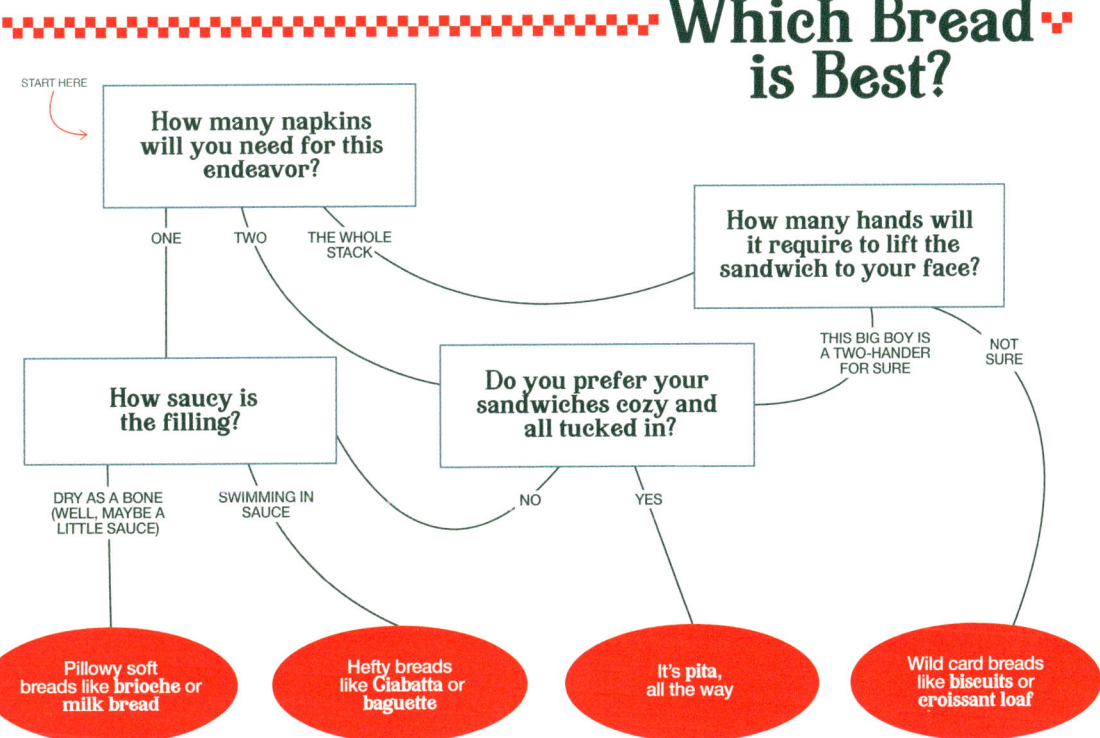

MORNING

We know, we know. Nobody has time in the morning. Eating, much less *cooking* breakfast can feel like an impossible task at 7 a.m. That's the whole reason morning sandwiches were invented. They are fast, cheap, and easy to pick up on your way to work (or, *ahem* . . . on your way home). They can also be conveniently eaten with just one hand, leaving the other free to spam your friends with memes.

In the recipes that follow, you'll find our take on the classics, like the Pancake Griddle (page 11), which is sausage, egg, and cheese at its best, but we go far beyond the basics here. A savory Chilaquiles Torta (page 20) will fill your gullet with what we can only describe as a symphony of carne asada, crispy tortilla chips, egg, beans, and queso fresco on a bolillo roll. We even have a recipe for Green Eggs and Ham (page 27) for all you Dr. Seuss–heads out there. You can eat this one while on a plane that's bound for Spain, or in your robe at your abode, among other places.

Above all, know that these sandwiches can be eaten at any time of day. But if you *do* happen to pull it together enough to make one of these before noon, then you get a gold star—the early idiot catches the worm, after all.

Cajun Breakfast Sandwich   3

Sam Scow's Favorite Version of
Elvis Presley's Favorite Sandwich   4

Chili Spiced French Toast Sandwich   7

Full English Breakfast   9

Pancake Griddle   11

Mumbai Masala Toast   14

French Onion Omelet Sandwich   16

Whitefish Salad Sandwich   19

Chilaquiles Torta   20

Everything Chopped on an
Everything Bagel   23

Korean Street Toast   25

Green Eggs and Ham   27

Garam Masala Eggs   28

Pork Roll   31

Hong Kong–Style Egg Sandwich   32

Shakshuka Sandwich   35

Fried Chicken Biscuit   37

Steak and Eggs   41

Bacon Jam and Chile Egg Biscuit   43

Chopped Sausage Sandwich   47

Turkey Breakfast Club   48

Pastrami Egg and Cheese   51

CAJUN BREAKFAST SANDWICH

Makes 2 sandwiches
Prep Time: 15 minutes
Cook Time: 10 minutes

INGREDIENTS

Croissants:
2 large croissants

Olive oil

Kosher salt

Ham:
8 ounces Tasso ham, thinly sliced, or substitute with smoked sliced deli ham or andouille sausage

Pinch of Old Bay Seasoning

Pinch of ground black pepper

Fried Eggs:
1 tablespoon olive oil

1 tablespoon unsalted butter

2 large eggs

Kosher salt

Pinch of Old Bay Seasoning

Sandwich Assembly:
¼ cup Spicy Cajun Mayo (page 201)

2 croissant sized pieces of romaine lettuce

4 slices of a large tomato (¼ inch thick)

2 to 4 cheddar cheese slices

The funny thing about Tasso ham, which is a major component of this recipe, is it's not technically ham—ham comes from the leg of the pig, and Tasso comes from the shoulder. It's spicier, smokier, and saltier, too. Leave it to the Cajuns to expand and improve upon our preconceived notions of pork. The Spicy Cajun Mayo adds the perfect zing to accompany all that "ham." However, unlike some other parts of this sandwich that we know, its name is quite accurate, so if you don't like spice, consider yourself warned.

INSTRUCTIONS

Heat up the Croissants:
1. Heat a large nonstick skillet over medium-high heat. Cut the croissants in half, drizzle the cut side with olive oil, and sprinkle with salt. Place cut side down in the skillet and cook for about 1 minute, until golden brown. Remove from the skillet and set aside.

Cook the Ham:
2. Increase the heat under the same skillet to high and add the ham in a single layer. Season with Old Bay Seasoning and pepper.
3. Cook until crispy, about 3 minutes, then flip and cook for another 2 minutes. Remove from the skillet and place the cheese slices on top to warm. Set aside.

Cook the Eggs:
4. Lower heat to medium and add the olive oil and butter. Once the butter has melted and is bubbling, season with salt and Old Bay Seasoning.
5. Crack the eggs into the pan. Baste the eggs with melted butter until the whites are cooked and the yolks are set, about 4 minutes.

Build the Sandwiches:
6. Start by spreading Spicy Cajun Mayo on the cut sides of both croissant halves. On the bottom half of the croissant, place romaine lettuce, two slices of tomato, Tasso ham, cheddar cheese, and a fried egg. Finish with the top half of the croissant.

SAM SCOW'S FAVORITE VERSION OF ELVIS PRESLEY'S FAVORITE SANDWICH

Makes 4 sandwiches
Prep Time: 5 minutes
Cook Time: 20 minutes

INGREDIENTS

Bacon, Bananas, and Eggs:

8 slices thick-cut maple bacon

3 tablespoons unsalted butter, separated

2 firm bananas, sliced on the bias ½ inch thick

Kosher salt

4 large eggs

Ground black pepper

Sandwich Assembly:

8 slices croissant bread

1 cup creamy peanut butter

Powdered sugar, for dusting

Everyone knows that Elvis's favorite sandwich is peanut butter, bacon, and banana. Sam Scow, the winner of our *Idiot Sandwich* breakfast competition, took it a step further by adding an egg and croissant bread. We'll never know for sure if Elvis would have approved, but we do know that everyone in our test kitchen began gyrating out of control when they tasted it. We're all shook up. Proceed with caution.

INSTRUCTIONS

Cook the Bacon:

1. In a large skillet, cook the bacon over medium heat until crispy, flipping as needed, about 10 minutes. Remove from the skillet and let rest on a paper towel–lined plate.

Caramelize the Bananas:

2. Wipe the skillet and increase the heat under the skillet to medium-high. Add 1 tablespoon of the butter, and once melted, add the sliced bananas in a single layer and lightly season with salt.

3. Cook the bananas for about 2 minutes on each side, until they turn golden brown and caramelize but still hold their shape. Remove the bananas from the skillet and set aside. Wipe the pan clean and set aside to be used for toasting the bread.

Fry the Eggs:

4. Heat a small nonstick skillet over medium heat. Add 1½ teaspoons of the remaining butter to the skillet. Once the butter has melted and is bubbling, crack 2 eggs into the pan and fry the eggs until the whites are set, about 3 to 4 minutes.

5. Cover with lid, if needed, to finish cooking so the yolks stay runny when the whites are set. Season with salt and pepper, then remove the eggs to a plate and repeat with the remaining 2 eggs.

Toast the Bread:

6. Return the large skillet to the stovetop over medium heat and melt the remaining 1 tablespoon butter. Spread the peanut butter on the bottom inside half of the 2 slices of bread.
7. Place the bottom half in the skillet, peanut butter side up, along with 2 more slices of bread; these will be your sandwich tops. Toast the bread until golden and crisp on the outside, then remove from the pan to continue assembly.

Build the Sandwiches:

8. Start with the bottom half of the bread already spread with peanut butter. Layer on two slices of bacon, caramelized bananas, and a fried egg. Top with the other half of the bread and sprinkle with a dusting of powdered sugar.

CHILI SPICED FRENCH TOAST SANDWICH

Makes 2 sandwiches
Prep Time: 25 minutes
Cook Time: 15 minutes

INGREDIENTS

Soft-Boiled Eggs:

4 large eggs

French Toast:

6 large eggs

¼ cup whole milk

1 teaspoon ground cinnamon

1 teaspoon vanilla extract

1 teaspoon ancho chile powder

1 tablespoon granulated sugar

½ teaspoon kosher salt

4 slices challah loaf, sliced ¼ inch thick

2 tablespoons unsalted butter

4 slices pepper jack cheese

Sandwich Assembly:

6 slices Hot Honey Bacon (page 206)

Maple syrup

> **NOTES FOR THE IDIOTS**
>
> Adding vinegar to your pot of water when boiling eggs makes the eggs easier to peel.

Spicy plus sweet plus pork equals delicious is not a new type of math. It's been around since the first person doused a pepperoni pizza with hot honey, back when Brooklyn hipsters ruled the food scene, circa 2010. This is basically our version of that, except instead of pepperoni we use bacon. And we substitute French toast for the pizza dough. And we also add eggs. Okay, our recipe is not at all like the pizza, but we do include hot honey, so there.

INSTRUCTIONS

Prepare the Soft-Boiled Eggs:

1. Bring a medium pot of water to a full boil. Gently add eggs to the pot and boil for 7 minutes. When finished cooking, transfer the eggs to a bowl of ice water and leave for 5 to 10 minutes to cool. Peel and slice each egg into thirds and set aside.

Make the French Toast:

2. Heat a large skillet over medium-low heat. In a shallow dish, beat together the eggs, milk, cinnamon, vanilla, ancho chile powder, sugar, and salt. Soak each slice of challah in the egg mixture, turning to coat.

3. Melt 1 tablespoon of the butter in the skillet. Add 2 soaked challah slices to the skillet and cook until golden brown, about 2 minutes, then flip. Top each slice with pepper jack cheese and cook for another 2 minutes so the outside is golden and the cheese is melted, then remove from pan for assembly. Repeat with the remaining challah slices.

Build the Sandwiches:

4. Start with a slice of challah, melted cheese facing up. Layer on three slices of the Hot Honey Bacon and six slices of egg. Place the top slice of challah on top, melted cheese facing down. Press the sandwich together and serve with maple syrup.

FULL ENGLISH BREAKFAST

Makes 2 sandwiches
Prep Time: 30 minutes
Cook Time: 45 minutes

INGREDIENTS

Mushrooms:
2 large portobello mushroom caps, cleaned

1 tablespoon olive oil

Roasted Tomato Smear:
8 plum tomatoes, halved

3 tablespoons neutral oil

Beans:
One 13.7-ounce can baked beans, such as Heinz

⅛ teaspoon onion powder

½ teaspoon sugar

Sandwich Assembly:
2 tablespoons neutral oil

2 bangers or regular link sausages, cut in half lengthwise

4 pieces back bacon or Canadian bacon

4 slices toasted English muffin bread

2 large eggs

1 tablespoon unsalted butter

Kosher salt

Ground black pepper

The Brits are world-renowned for their horrifying food—just ask anyone who's ever been served a stargazy pie. (Don't google it, don't you dare google it.) Nevertheless, we wanted to include an ode to our fearless leader—hey, Gordon!—so, we've transformed the quintessential English fry-up into a sandwich any idiot will love. We did you a favor by omitting the black pudding, but you'll have to pry the baked beans out of our cold dead hands. Or in this case, your mouth.

INSTRUCTIONS

Roast the Mushrooms:
1. Preheat the oven to 400°F. Line a sheet tray with parchment paper. Place the mushrooms on the prepared sheet tray and toss with the olive oil, a generous pinch of salt, and pepper. Roast for 20 to 30 minutes, or until browned and tender.

Make the Roasted Tomato Smear:
2. While the mushrooms are in the oven, line another sheet tray with parchment paper. Place the tomatoes on the sheet tray, toss with the neutral oil, and season with salt. Roast for 20 to 30 minutes, or until golden brown.

3. Let cool to room temperature, then transfer to a blender and blend until the tomatoes are broken down and spreadable but still chunky. Add salt to taste.

Heat up the Beans:
4. While the mushrooms and tomatoes roast, combine the beans, onion powder, sugar, and a pinch of black pepper and salt in a small pot. Heat over medium-low heat for about 10 minutes, stirring frequently. Adjust the seasoning to taste and reserve on the stove over the lowest heat to keep warm for assembly.

Cook the Bangers:
5. Heat the neutral oil in a medium skillet over medium-high heat. Add the bangers and cook on all sides until caramelized, about 8 minutes total. Add a splash of water, cover, and steam for 5 minutes, or until cooked through and their internal temperature reaches 145°F. Remove the bangers from the pan and set them aside. Wipe the pan out with a paper towel.

continued

Fry the Bacon:

6. Cut four ¼-inch slits on opposite sides of the bacon to prevent it from curling.
7. Heat the wiped-out pan over medium heat. Add the bacon and fry until crispy, about 2 minutes per side. Set the bacon aside and wipe the pan out again.

Fry the Eggs:

8. Heat ½ tablespoon of butter in a small nonstick skillet over medium heat. When the butter bubbles up and the foam subsides, crack 2 eggs into the pan and fry them for 3 to 4 minutes, until the whites are set. Cover with lid, if needed, to finish cooking so the yolks stay runny when the whites are set. Season with salt and pepper, then remove the eggs from the skillet. Repeat with the other 2 eggs.

Build the Sandwiches:

9. Start with the bottom slice of toasted English muffin bread, then layer on ¼ cup of beans, a portobello mushroom cap, two slices of bacon, two halves of bangers, and a fried egg. Spread the top slice of the English muffin bread with Roasted Tomato Smear and place it on top.

NOTES FOR THE IDIOTS

Speed things up by roasting the mushrooms and the tomatoes at the same time, in different pans. Or skip the roasted tomato smear altogether and use sun-dried tomatoes instead.

Back bacon, also known as rashers, is a British cut of bacon from the pork loin. It is leaner than American bacon and similar to Canadian bacon. Purchase at a British market or online.

PANCAKE GRIDDLE

Makes 4 sandwiches
Prep Time: 20 minutes
Cook Time: 45 minutes

Picture this, it's the year 2000. The Earth survived Y2K, but the McDonald's execs recognized a new problem on the horizon. It was a glaring hole in their breakfast menu—a dearth of sweet, portable options. Thus, work on the McGriddle began. According to the person who invented it (and we are not making this up), the biggest obstacle was figuring out a way to get *syrup crystals inside* the hotcakes for optimal portability, i.e., no one wants maple syrup dripping down their arm as they board the train for work. After years of trial and error, the McGriddle debuted in 2003 to immediate success, syrup crystals and all.

Our version does not include syrup crystals, but we like it even better because we drizzle real maple syrup right into the hotcakes as they cook. This makes for a portable, and dare we say tastier, version of the most famous breakfast sandwich in the world.

INGREDIENTS

Spicy Maple Mustard:
3 tablespoons maple syrup

¼ cup spicy brown mustard or whole grain mustard

Pinch of cayenne pepper, optional

Maple Pancakes:
1½ cups all-purpose flour

2 tablespoons granulated sugar

½ teaspoon kosher salt

3½ teaspoons baking powder

1 large egg, at room temperature

3 tablespoons melted butter or neutral oil

1 cup buttermilk or whole milk

1 teaspoon vanilla extract

8 tablespoons maple syrup, separated

2 tablespoons unsalted butter

Cooking spray or additional unsalted butter for greasing round cutters

Sausage Patties:
4 pork breakfast sausage patties, each patty 1 to 2 ounces, or substitute any breakfast protein

2 teaspoons neutral oil

4 slices American cheese

Eggs:
4 large eggs

Unsalted butter

Kosher salt

Ground black pepper

Sandwich Assembly:
Maple syrup, for serving

continued

INSTRUCTIONS

Prepare the Spicy Maple Mustard:

1. In a small bowl, mix the maple syrup, mustard, and cayenne until thoroughly combined and reserve for assembly.

Make the Maple Pancakes:

2. In a medium bowl, sift together the flour, sugar, salt, and baking powder. In a separate bowl, whisk the egg until fluffy and fully combined, about 1 to 2 minutes. Add the melted butter, buttermilk, and vanilla to the whisked egg. Slowly whisk the dry ingredients into the egg mixture until fully combined; some lumps are fine, and the batter will be thick. Set aside.

3. Heat a medium nonstick skillet or griddle over medium heat and lightly coat with butter. Grease the inside of a 4-inch biscuit ring cutter and place it on the pan to warm for 30 seconds. Pour ¼ cup of batter into the ring mold. Once the edges start to set, about 1 minute, pour 1 tablespoon of the maple syrup into the center and lightly swirl into the batter with a toothpick. The batter will rise as it cooks for another 1 to 2 minutes. Remove the ring mold, flip the pancake, and cook until golden brown, about another 2 minutes.

4. Remove cooked pancakes from the pan and set aside. Once the pancakes have cooled slightly, slice in half lengthwise and reserve for assembly. Repeat with the remaining batter to make 8 pancakes.

Cook the Sausage Patties:

5. While pancakes are cooking, heat a medium nonstick skillet over medium heat and lightly grease with oil. Add the sausage patties to the pan and cook for 3 to 5 minutes on each side, until cooked through and caramelized. Top with a cheese slice and let it melt; use a lid to cover the pan and speed up the melting process if needed. Remove from the heat and reserve for assembly.

Cook the Eggs:

6. Heat a medium nonstick skillet over medium heat and lightly coat the pan with a thin layer of butter. Grease the inside of a 3-inch biscuit ring cutter with butter or cooking spray and warm the ring cutter in the pan for 30 seconds. Crack one egg into the center of the ring cutter and season with salt and pepper. Cook for about 3 minutes so the edges set, then remove the ring cutter and cover with a lid so the egg cooks through, about 2 minutes. Remove from the heat and repeat with the remaining eggs.

Build the Sandwiches:

7. Start with the bottom half of the sliced maple pancake and spread on the Spicy Maple Mustard. Layer the sausage patty with melted cheese, followed by the egg. Top with the other half of the maple pancake and serve with maple syrup.

NOTES FOR THE IDIOTS

If you are in a time crunch, substitute boxed pancake mix to make the pancakes, following the instructions on the box to prepare the batter. Follow our cooking technique when it comes time to cook them, and most importantly, don't forget to add the maple syrup drizzle while cooking.

Heads up—you'll need both a 4-inch and 3-inch stainless steel ring or biscuit cutter to properly make this recipe. They can be purchased online and are quite affordable.

MUMBAI MASALA TOAST

Makes 4 sandwiches
Prep Time: 25 minutes
Cook Time: 30 minutes

Mumbai masala toast is a popular street food from, you guessed it, Mumbai. It typically consists of masala-spiked potatoes and green chutney layered between bread and toasted to perfection. We like to dip ours in an herbaceous batter before we toast it, and we also add way too much cheese.

INGREDIENTS

Spiced Mashed Potatoes:

1 pound Yukon gold potatoes, peeled and cut into even medium-sized pieces

¾ teaspoon kosher salt, plus more for cooking the potatoes and to taste

1 teaspoon unsalted butter

¾ teaspoon garam masala

Herb Batter:

6 large eggs

3½ tablespoons chopped fresh cilantro

3 tablespoons finely diced red onion

2 scallions, green parts only, sliced

1 teaspoon kosher salt

½ teaspoon ground turmeric

1 cup shredded pepper jack cheese

Sandwich Assembly:

8 slices sprouted wheat bread

8 slices pepper jack cheese

Coriander Chutney (page 197), or substitute with store-bought

1 large tomato, cut into 8 thin slices

2 tablespoons unsalted butter

INSTRUCTIONS

Make the Spiced Mashed Potatoes:

1. Place the potatoes in a medium pot of cold, liberally salted water. Bring to a boil over high heat, then lower the heat and simmer for 20 minutes, or until easily pierced with a fork. Be mindful not to overboil!
2. Drain the potatoes and mash them with a potato masher. The mashed potatoes should still have some lumps for texture. Add the butter, garam masala, and salt. Adjust the seasoning to taste. Set aside for assembly.

Prepare the Herb Batter:

3. Crack the eggs into a medium bowl and whisk until foamy. Add the cilantro, onions, scallions, salt, turmeric, and grated cheese. Mix well and reserve.

Cook the Sandwiches:

4. Preheat a griddle or large sauté pan over medium-low heat.
5. Lay the slices of bread on a flat surface. Place 2 slices of the jack cheese on half of the slices. Spread 1 to 2 tablespoons of Coriander Chutney on the remaining slices. Spoon about ⅓ cup of spiced potatoes onto the bottom halves, spreading evenly to the edges. Add 2 slices of tomato on top of the spiced potatoes. Sandwich the two halves together, pressing the two layers.
6. Coat the hot pan in butter and dip each sandwich into the egg batter, ensuring it's well coated, then place on the griddle (work in batches if necessary). Cook one side for 4 to 5 minutes, until deep golden brown. Carefully flip and cook the other side for another 4 to 5 minutes, until the cheese is melted on the inside and the batter on the outside is golden. Serve with additional Coriander Chutney.

> **NOTES FOR THE IDIOTS**
>
> Instead of making the spiced mashed potatoes from scratch, simply stir the garam masala into some leftover mashed potatoes and call it a day.

FRENCH ONION OMELET SANDWICH

Makes 2 sandwiches
Prep Time: 25 minutes
Cook Time: 45 minutes

INGREDIENTS

French-Style Caramelized Onions:

1½ tablespoons extra-virgin olive oil

3 cups sliced yellow onions

1 tablespoon sherry vinegar

1 tablespoon fresh thyme leaves, chopped

Omelets:

8 large eggs

2 tablespoons unsalted butter

½ cup shredded Gruyère or Swiss cheese

Gruyère Toast:

4 slices brioche

1 tablespoon unsalted butter, softened

4 slices Gruyère or Swiss cheese

¼ cup all-purpose flour

Sandwich Assembly:

Whole Grain Mustard Mayo (page 202)

Kosher salt

Ground black pepper

They say the mark of a true chef is whether they can make a proper French omelet. We say the mark of a true idiot is whether they can make a proper French onion omelet *sandwich*.

Follow the instructions explicitly to pull it off: Caramelize the onions with sherry vinegar for that classic French onion je ne sais quoi. Dredge the cheese in flour so it sticks to the bread more easily as it melts. Tilt the pan to 45 degrees when you fold the omelet to get gravity on your side. Only then will you be able to truly master the French onion omelet sandwich, and answer that age-old question: "Am I an idiot?" Yes, Chef, you are.

INSTRUCTIONS

Caramelize the Onions:

1. Heat a large sauté pan over medium heat and add the olive oil. Add the sliced onions and cook for about 5 minutes, until softened. Reduce the heat to medium-low and stir consistently for 20 to 30 minutes, until the onions have a deep caramel color. Adding a small amount of water as the onions begin to brown will help them caramelize evenly.

2. Once your onions are a deep golden brown, add the vinegar, thyme, a pinch of salt, and pepper and cook until the vinegar dissipates, about 5 minutes. Adjust the seasoning to taste.

Make the Gruyère Toast:

3. Preheat a large nonstick skillet over medium heat. Lightly spread the butter on both sides of the bread slices. Lightly dredge one side of the cheese in flour.

4. Working two bread slices at a time, place the cheese, flour side down, in the pan and top with a bread slice. Cook for 3 to 5 minutes, until the cheese melts and then becomes slightly crisp and golden. The cheese will continue to crisp once removed from the heat. Flip the sandwich and toast the non-cheese side for about 2 minutes, until golden brown. Remove and set aside with the cheese side facing up. Repeat for the second sandwich bread slices.

Make the Omelets:

5. Heat a small nonstick skillet over medium heat. Add 1 tablespoon of the butter to the pan and let it melt and completely coat the pan. Crack the eggs into a bowl, whisk, pour half of the whisked eggs into the pan and cook for about 30 seconds, until the eggs begin to set.

6. Use a spatula to gently push the set edges toward the center, allowing the raw egg to flow into open spaces. This will begin to resemble scrambled eggs but will still be lying mostly flat in the pan as you continue to push the cooked eggs around. Continue until the eggs are mostly cooked and almost set. Season the eggs with a pinch of salt and pepper and add half of the shredded cheese on one half of the omelet. Tilt the pan at a 45-degree angle and begin folding the egg over itself in half. Remove from pan and set aside for assembly. Repeat the above steps for the second omelet.

Build the Sandwiches:

7. Begin by spreading Whole Grain Mustard Mayo on the inside of both cheese toasts. On one half, with the cheese side facing down, layer caramelized onions and an omelet. Place the other half on top, with the cheese side facing out.

WHITEFISH SALAD SANDWICH

Makes 4 sandwiches
Prep Time: 30 minutes
Cook Time: 5 minutes

INGREDIENTS

Whitefish Salad:

8 ounces smoked whitefish, or substitute with any hot smoked fish

¾ cup mayonnaise

½ cup finely diced celery

½ cup finely diced red onion

3 tablespoons finely chopped fresh dill

1 tablespoon fresh lemon juice

¼ teaspoon ground black pepper

Kosher salt

Sandwich Assembly:

8 slices marbled rye bread, toasted

1 English cucumber, sliced into rounds

Horseradish Cream Cheese (page 196)

Whitefish salad is perhaps the most ubiquitous appetizer found in the Jewish delis of America, and for good reason—it's freaking delicious. It consists of lightly smoked, flaky whitefish mixed with a touch of mayonnaise, finely chopped celery, onion, and dill. We like to eat ours with a sizable dollop of Horseradish Cream Cheese, sandwiched between toasted rye bread, but this also goes great on a bagel.

INSTRUCTIONS

Prepare the Whitefish Salad:

1. Remove the skin and bones from the whitefish, then flake the fish into a medium bowl. Add the mayonnaise, celery, red onion, dill, lemon juice, and pepper. Season with salt and refrigerate until ready to assemble.

Build the Sandwiches:

2. Lay down a slice of toasted marbled rye bread and spread with Horseradish Cream Cheese. Spoon ½ cup of whitefish salad on top, then add six to eight cucumber slices. Finish with the second slice of marbled rye bread.

CHILAQUILES TORTA

Makes 4 sandwiches
Prep Time: 25 minutes
Cook Time: 30 minutes

Chilaquiles are proof that Mexicans know how to make the best breakfast in the world, and their invention dates all the way back to the ancient Aztecs. The name roughly translates to "chili water," and they were created as a way to use up stale tortillas. The goal is to smother crispy fried tortillas in just enough sauce (aka chili water), for just long enough that they become soft in the middle yet retain their crispy edges. Carne asada is not traditionally involved, but you know how we like to amp things up around here, and of course we always add bread. Throw it on a bolillo roll and you'll be spreading the gospel of the Chilaquiles Torta in no time.

INGREDIENTS

Carne Asada:

½ cup fresh lime juice, from about 4 limes

½ cup fresh orange juice, from about 1 orange

¼ cup olive oil

4 large garlic cloves, chopped

½ teaspoon dried Mexican oregano

1 teaspoon ground cumin

1 teaspoon ground coriander

1 teaspoon ancho chile powder

1 teaspoon kosher salt

2 pounds flank or skirt steak

Chilaquiles:

1 cup neutral oil

6 taco-sized corn tortillas, cut into 6 triangles, or substitute with store-bought tortilla chips

½ small white onion, diced

Salsa Verde (page 196), or substitute with store-bought

8 ounces Oaxaca or Monterey Jack cheese, shredded

Sandwich Assembly:

4 tablespoons (½ stick) cold unsalted butter, cut into pats

8 large eggs

4 bolillo rolls, halved lengthwise and warmed

¼ cup picked cilantro leaves

½ cup queso fresco

½ cup Mexican crema

One 16-ounce can refried beans, warmed and seasoned with salt and pepper

INSTRUCTIONS

Cook the Carne Asada:

1. In a large bowl, whisk together the lime juice, orange juice, olive oil, garlic, oregano, cumin, coriander, chile powder, and salt. Add the steak to the marinade, cover, and let it marinate for 30 minutes. Heat a grill pan or sauté pan over medium-high heat. Place the steak on the grill and cook until a caramelized crust forms, about 5 minutes. Flip and caramelize the other side and continue cooking to your desired doneness. Remove from the heat and let rest for 5 minutes, then thinly slice and reserve until assembly.

Make the Chilaquiles:

2. In a large pot, heat 1 cup of the oil over medium-high heat to 350°F. Fry the tortillas in batches, stirring continuously, until golden brown and crispy, about 3 minutes. Remove the tortilla chips to a wire rack or paper towel–lined tray to drain excess oil.

3. Transfer 2 tablespoons of the frying oil to a large sauté pan and heat over medium heat. Add the onion and cook until translucent, about 5 minutes. Add the Salsa Verde and fried tortilla chips, tossing to coat. Remove from the heat, sprinkle with the shredded cheese, and reserve for assembly.

Fry the Eggs:

4. In a small skillet over medium-high heat, melt 1 tablespoon of the butter. Crack 2 eggs into the skillet and cook until the edges are crisp and the whites are set, 3 to 4 minutes. Baste the whites with the butter in the pan or cover with lid, if needed, to finish cooking so the yolks stay runny when the whites are set.

Build the Sandwiches

5. Begin with the bottom half of the bolillo roll. Add a layer of refried beans, followed by piled chilaquiles, carne asada, and two fried eggs. Drizzle with crema, then sprinkle with queso fresco crumbles and cilantro. Top with the other half of the bolillo roll.

EVERYTHING CHOPPED ON AN EVERYTHING BAGEL

Makes 4 sandwiches
Prep Time: 12 minutes
Cook Time: 5 minutes

INGREDIENTS

Scallion Cream Cheese:

(or substitute with a store-bought savory cream cheese)

8 ounces cream cheese, at room temperature

4 scallions, thinly sliced

Zest of 1 lemon

½ teaspoon fresh lemon juice

Chopped Gravlax:

4 ounces gravlax

1 tablespoon capers in brine, drained

2 slices of seeded Roma tomato

2 slices of thinly sliced red onion

Arugula Mix:

1 cup arugula

Zest of ¼ lemon

Juice of ½ lemon

1 tablespoon extra-virgin olive oil

Sandwich Assembly:

4 everything bagels, sliced in half lengthwise and toasted

Kosher salt

Ground black pepper

Talk about bang for your buck. This one is so easy to make, we hesitate to even call it a recipe. Basically, you take all the best parts of a bagel and lox, chop it all together, and mix it with a hefty amount of scallion cream cheese, then smear it back on the bagel (which you toasted while you were doing all that chopping).

INSTRUCTIONS

Make the Scallion Cream Cheese:

1. In a medium bowl, soften the cream cheese using a rubber spatula. Add the scallions, lemon zest and juice, a pinch of salt, and pepper. Mix until well combined. Remove ¼ cup of the mixture and reserve for assembly.

Make the Chopped Gravlax:

2. Place the gravlax, capers, tomatoes, and onions on a clean cutting board. Roughly chop the ingredients together. Add the chopped mixture to the bowl with the remaining scallion cream cheese and fold together gently with a rubber spatula until evenly combined.

Prepare the Arugula Mix:

3. In a separate bowl, toss the arugula with the lemon zest, juice, and olive oil. Season with a pinch of salt and pepper.

Build the Sandwiches:

4. Start with the bottom half of the bagel and spread on scallion cream cheese. Add the chopped gravlax mixture, followed by a handful of arugula mix. Finish with the top half of the bagel.

KOREAN STREET TOAST

Makes 2 sandwiches
Prep Time: 20 minutes
Cook Time: 15 minutes

INGREDIENTS

Vegetable Egg Patty:

4 large eggs

1 teaspoon kosher salt

1½ cups julienned green cabbage

1½ cups shredded carrots (about 2 medium carrots)

⅔ cup julienned yellow onion

⅓ cup scallions, finely cut

1 tablespoon unsalted butter

Sandwich Assembly:

4 slices American cheese

4 slices white bread, toasted

Spicy Ketchup (page 203), or substitute with store-bought spicy ketchup

Korean street toast, also known as *gilgeori*, roughly translates to "roadside toast." The filling is technically an omelet, but in reality it's more like a bonkers amount of crisp, savory vegetables that are just barely held together by eggs. If you were to eat one of these in South Korea, they'd probably throw a little sugar in with the ketchup, but we threw in gochujang instead for extra flavor, and also for fun because gochujang is delicious. Not only will this get you up and running in the morning, but it's an excellent way to get your veggies in.

INSTRUCTIONS

Make the Vegetable Egg Patty:

1. Heat a medium nonstick pan over medium heat. In a medium bowl, crack the eggs and whisk in the salt. Add the cabbage, carrots, onion, and scallions; mix thoroughly. Add 1½ teaspoons of the butter to the pan and let it melt and bubble.

2. Pour half of the egg mixture into the pan and cook for 10 to 20 seconds, until it starts to coagulate. Using a spatula, start shaping the egg into a rectangle about double the length of your bread slice. Cook for another 1½ minutes, then flip and cook for an additional 1½ minutes, or until fully cooked through.

3. Add two slices of cheese and melt over egg patty.

4. Cut the rectangular egg patty into two squares, stack them on top of each other, and set aside for sandwich assembly. Repeat the process with the remaining egg mixture to make a second stacked patty.

Build the Sandwiches:

5. Slather Spicy Ketchup on two slices of bread. Place one stacked vegetable egg patty on a slice, then top with the other slice of bread to form a sandwich.

NOTES FOR THE IDIOTS

Throw some cooked ham or bacon on top of that egg patty for a meatier version of this sando.

GREEN EGGS AND HAM

Makes 2 sandwiches
Prep Time: 25 minutes
Cook Time: 20 minutes

INGREDIENTS

Maple-Glazed Ham:

1 teaspoon neutral oil

2 slices thick-cut country ham steak, cut in half to fit the rolls

2 tablespoons maple syrup

Pesto Scrambled Eggs:

5 large eggs

2 tablespoons unsalted butter

4 tablespoons Pesto (page 199), or substitute with store-bought

½ cup chopped Swiss chard leaves or baby spinach

2 tablespoons crème fraîche or sour cream

Pinch of kosher salt

Pinch of ground black pepper

Sandwich Assembly:

2 poppy seed kaiser rolls, cut in half and toasted

¼ cup ricotta cheese

Look here, we've made green eggs and ham! We've made it quickly, in a pan. We hope you like it (and you should). It took so long to make it good. Many versions we did try, we even made one on some rye. But then we realized, in our haste, the only way for this to taste . . . is if we add some pesto here, and then some syrup, over there. We put it on a kaiser roll, and had our office take a poll. They loved it all, no vote was split, so here it is, ya idiot.

INSTRUCTIONS

Make the Maple-Glazed Ham:

1. Heat a nonstick skillet over medium-high heat and add the oil. Once the oil is shimmering, add the ham slices and cook through for about 1½ minutes on each side to caramelize.

2. Pour in the maple syrup to coat the ham slices and cook for another 30 seconds on each side to glaze the ham. Remove the ham from the pan and set aside. Wipe the pan clean.

Cook the Pesto Scrambled Eggs:

3. Lower the heat under the skillet to medium. Add the butter to the skillet, and once melted stir in the Swiss chard to wilt for about 3 minutes. You can cover the pan with a lid to help wilt if needed.

4. In a large bowl, whisk the eggs until the yolks and whites are combined, then pour the whisked eggs into a pan. Using a rubber spatula, push the eggs around in the pan as they cook and coagulate. When the eggs are halfway cooked, add the pesto, stirring to combine. When the eggs are just about fully cooked but still are slightly liquid and soft, turn off the heat and fold in the crème fraîche. Season with the salt and pepper.

Build the Sandwiches:

5. Begin by spreading ricotta on the inside of both halves of the seeded kaiser roll. On the bottom half, layer the maple-glazed ham and pesto scrambled eggs, then top with the other half of the roll.

GARAM MASALA EGGS

Makes 2 sandwiches
Prep Time: 10 minutes
Cook Time: 25 minutes

This is a super easy, flavor-packed breakfast for those of you who are busy but still like to eat your eggs with style. You can make the yogurt and onions the night before, so all you'll need to do is zombie walk to the kitchen to make quick work of scrambling up the eggs. The golden onions and garam masala bring the aromatics and the pillowy soft naan will make you yearn to eat this sandwich back in bed where you belong.

INGREDIENTS

Mint Yogurt:
½ cup plain yogurt

1 tablespoon finely chopped fresh mint

¼ teaspoon ground turmeric

Golden Onions:
2 tablespoons unsalted butter

2 tablespoons olive oil

1 teaspoon yellow mustard seeds

1 teaspoon cumin seeds

1 small yellow onion, sliced

6 ounces (2 large handfuls) baby spinach

Spiced Scrambled Eggs:
2 tablespoons unsalted butter

1 tablespoon olive oil

1 teaspoon garam masala

1 teaspoon ground turmeric

1 cup baby spinach leaves

4 large eggs, whisked

Sandwich Assembly:
2 pieces naan bread

1 tablespoon unsalted butter, softened

Kosher salt

INSTRUCTIONS

Prepare the Mint Yogurt:

1. In a medium bowl, whisk together the yogurt, mint, turmeric, and a pinch of salt. Set aside and reserve for assembly.

Cook the Onions:

2. In a medium skillet, heat the butter and olive oil over medium heat until the butter melts. Add the mustard seeds and cumin seeds and cook until fragrant, about 1 minute. Add sliced onions and cook until tender and golden brown, about 10 to 15 minutes.
3. Stir in the spinach and cook until it begins to wilt, about 3 minutes, then season with a pinch of salt. Remove the mixture from the skillet and set aside.

Cook the Eggs:

4. Return the skillet to medium heat and add the butter and olive oil. Once the butter melts, add the garam masala and turmeric, stirring to combine and toast lightly.
5. In a small bowl, whisk the eggs, then pour into pan and gently stir until cooked through and fluffy, 3 to 5 minutes. Season with a pinch of salt.
6. Remove from the heat and stir in the golden onion and spinach mixture. Wipe the pan clean and return to the heat.

Toast the Naan:

7. Lather the naan with the butter. Toast in the clean skillet over medium heat until light golden brown and warmed.

Build the Sandwiches:

8. Start with a toasted naan and spread a layer of mint yogurt across the entire piece. On one half of the naan, add a layer of half the golden onion, egg, and spinach mixture. Fold over and enjoy.

PORK ROLL

Makes 2 sandwiches
Prep Time: 5 minutes
Cook Time: 15 minutes

INGREDIENTS

Ham and Eggs:

8 slices Taylor ham

2 tablespoons unsalted butter

4 large eggs

Pinch of kosher salt

Pinch of ground black pepper

4 slices American cheese

Sandwich Assembly:

2 kaiser rolls, cut in half lengthwise

Unsalted butter, softened

Ketchup, for serving

NOTES FOR THE IDIOTS

If you can't get your mitts on Taylor ham, you're out of luck—there is no substitute for Taylor ham.

Just kidding, you could probably get by with a thick-cut deli ham or sliced ham steak. But, actually, that wouldn't be the same, so never mind, probably best just to stick with the Taylor ham.

This sandwich is Taylor ham, and Taylor ham is this sandwich. What we are trying to say is, it's all about the meat, and the entire state of New Jersey is invested. John Taylor of Trenton, New Jersey, invented Taylor ham in 1856, and whether to call it that or "pork roll" has been dividing the population of the Garden State ever since. More than one bar fight has erupted over this (we assume). There is one thing pretty much every citizen of Jersey can agree on, though, and that's when you slice it, griddle it, and eat it on a kaiser roll with egg and cheese, it's always called delicious.

INSTRUCTIONS

Cook the Ham:

1. Preheat a large skillet over medium heat. Use a sharp knife or scissors to cut 4 quarter-inch slits on opposite sides of the ham to prevent it from curling. Put the ham in the skillet and cook until lightly crisped and caramelized, about 90 seconds each side. Remove the ham from the pan and set aside for assembly.

Toast the Kaiser Rolls:

2. Butter the inside of the kaiser roll halves and place the cut side down in the pan to toast. Once toasted, remove and set aside for assembly.

Cook the Eggs:

3. In a small nonstick skillet, melt 1 tablespoon of the butter over medium-high heat. Crack 2 of the eggs into the skillet and cook until the whites are set and the edges are crispy. Season with the salt and pepper and top each egg with a slice of cheese so that it melts. Remove the eggs from the pan and repeat with the remaining eggs.

Build the Sandwiches:

4. Start with the bottom half of the kaiser roll. Layer on four slices of ham, followed by two cheese-covered eggs. Top with the other half of the roll and serve with ketchup.

HONG KONG–STYLE EGG SANDWICH

Makes 2 sandwiches

Prep Time: 5 minutes

Cook Time: 15 minutes

INGREDIENTS

Corned Beef:

1 tablespoon neutral oil

6 ounces deli corned beef, sliced

Hong Kong–Style Scrambled Eggs:

6 large eggs

6 tablespoons evaporated milk

2 teaspoons sesame oil, or substitute with neutral oil

2 teaspoons kosher salt

2 pinches of ground white pepper

2 teaspoons cornstarch

2 tablespoons neutral oil

Sandwich Assembly:

2 tablespoons unsalted butter

4 slices milk bread, cut ¼ inch thick and lightly toasted with butter on one side

Kewpie mayonnaise

Spicy Ketchup, optional (page 203)

The diners of Hong Kong are known, nay PRAISED, for their egg-cooking technique. There are many variations of this sandwich (we're going with corned beef here), but one thing always stays true—the eggs are stacked high in fluffy, custardy layers that melt in your mouth. The trick lies in the cornstarch. It retains the water that would naturally seep out of the eggs, giving them that signature creamy texture. As added insurance, we build this with the toasted side of the bread facing inward to help the sandwich keep its structure. But be warned: It *does* take some flair to cook the eggs right. Now, we idiots do a lot of things well, but more than anything, we've mastered the art of perseverance, so, if at first you don't succeed, try, try again.

INSTRUCTIONS

Cook the Corned Beef:

1. In the pan, heat the oil until it is shimmering. Add the corned beef and cook until crispy on both sides, about 90 seconds each side. Set the corned beef aside, wipe out the pan, and reduce the heat to medium-low.

Prepare the Hong Kong–Style Scrambled Eggs:

2. In a medium bowl, whisk together the eggs, evaporated milk, sesame oil, salt, and white pepper. In a separate small bowl, mix the cornstarch with 2 tablespoons water until smooth, then whisk it into the egg mixture.

3. Add half of the oil to the pan and heat until it is shimmering. Pour half of the egg mixture into the pan. Using a rubber spatula, push the egg mixture around to create cooked thin layers of egg, allowing the runny egg to spread onto the hot pan as you push the mixture. Turn off the heat and carefully flip the omelet to lightly cook the top side. The cooked egg should still look wet and glossy. Repeat the steps with the remaining egg and continue building the sandwich to serve immediately.

Build the Sandwiches:

4. Start by spreading Kewpie mayonnaise on the toasted side of a slice of milk bread. Top with the scrambled eggs, followed by the corned beef. Finish with the second slice of milk bread, and spread with the Spicy Ketchup.

NOTES FOR THE IDIOTS

Because milk bread is incredibly soft and light, we toast the inside of the slices, too. This prevents the eggs and sauces from sogging it out, and it adds a little bit of texture.

Once you've nailed the technique, use this as a base recipe to play with. Start by adding any of the sauces from our condiment chapter and work your way up from there.

This is *not* a case where you can sub your favorite style of cooked egg. The technique makes the sandwich.

SHAKSHUKA SANDWICH

Makes 4 sandwiches
Prep Time: 20 minutes
Cook Time: 35 minutes

INGREDIENTS

Tomato Pepper Sauce and Eggs:

¼ cup olive oil

1 cup diced onion

1 large red bell pepper, diced

2 large garlic cloves, sliced

1½ teaspoons kosher salt

1 teaspoon ground coriander

1½ tablespoons sweet paprika

2 teaspoons ground cumin

1½ tablespoons harissa paste or 2½ tablespoons harissa sauce

One 28-ounce can crushed tomatoes

8 large eggs

Sandwich Assembly:

Four 6-inch soft baguettes, cut in half hinge style

Parsley leaves, optional

¼ cup crumbled feta cheese

Whipped Feta (page 198)

> **NOTES FOR THE IDIOTS**
>
> The sauce can be made ahead of time and stored in the fridge for up to 4 days.

Shakshuka is a classic North African dish of eggs poached, not in water, but in a spiced stew of tomatoes, peppers, and onions. It makes for a tasty breakfast, so, on a hunch, we did what we do best—we sandwichified it. It's a little messier to eat than a traditional shakshuka, but if you do it right, you'll have perfectly poached yolks mixed with a piquant tomato sauce dripping down your chin in no time. Maybe grab a couple extra napkins for this one.

INSTRUCTIONS

Prepare the Tomato Pepper Sauce:

1. Heat the olive oil in a large sauté pan over medium heat. Add the onion and bell pepper and cook for 5 minutes, or until the onion is translucent and the pepper is softened.
2. Stir in the garlic, salt, coriander, paprika, cumin, and harissa paste and cook for an additional 1 minute, or until the garlic is golden and the spices are fragrant. Pour in the tomatoes, breaking them down with a large spoon. Bring to a simmer, and cook for 15 to 20 minutes to allow the flavors to combine. Adjust the seasoning to taste.

Poach the Eggs:

3. Use a large spoon to create small wells in the warm sauce and crack 1 egg into each well. Cook the eggs for 5 to 8 minutes, until the whites are set and the yolk is still runny. Cover with lid, if needed, to finish cooking so the yolks stay runny when the whites are set.

Build the Sandwiches:

4. Spread Whipped Feta on the bottom half of the baguette. Add a generous amount of tomato pepper sauce, followed by two poached eggs and feta crumbles. Sprinkle with parsley to finish, then close the baguette.

FRIED CHICKEN BISCUIT

Makes 6 sandwiches
Prep Time: 1 hour
Cook Time: 25 minutes

This one takes some foresight, but what you lose in spontaneity, you gain in moist yet crispy fried chicken doused in a spicy maple syrup and the flakiest biscuits in town. Brine the chicken at least one hour in advance, but ideally overnight to give it plenty of time for the flavor osmosis to set in, and freeze those biscuits before baking them (it helps retain said flakiness). Speaking of foresight, be sure to schedule yourself a nap after you eat this.

INGREDIENTS

Chicken Marinade:
1 cup pickle brine
1 cup buttermilk
1 teaspoon kosher salt
1 teaspoon chicken seasoning, optional
1 teaspoon smoked paprika
1 teaspoon garlic powder
1 teaspoon ground black pepper
2 pounds (6 pieces) boneless, skinless chicken thighs

Chicken Dredge:
2 cups all-purpose flour
½ cup cornstarch
1 tablespoon garlic powder
2 teaspoons kosher salt, plus more for finishing
2 teaspoons smoked paprika
½ teaspoon cayenne pepper, optional
¼ cup buttermilk
2 quarts neutral oil, for frying

Biscuits:
3 cups all-purpose flour
1 tablespoon baking powder
1 tablespoon granulated sugar
1½ teaspoons kosher salt
1 teaspoon baking soda
¾ cup (1½ sticks) unsalted butter, frozen
1¼ cups buttermilk
4 tablespoons (½ stick) unsalted butter, melted
2 tablespoons honey, optional

Hot Maple Syrup:
¼ cup maple syrup
2 tablespoons sriracha

Sandwich Assembly:
Pickle slices

> **NOTES FOR THE IDIOTS**
>
> If you are one of those psychopaths who likes to eat eggs and chicken together, like some sort of monster, this is your chance. Add a fried egg to this sandwich and go to town.
>
> Substitute store-bought biscuits for homemade in a pinch.

continued

INSTRUCTIONS

Marinate the Chicken:

1. In a large bowl, make the marinade by whisking together the pickle brine, buttermilk, salt, chicken seasoning, if using, smoked paprika, garlic powder, and black pepper. Submerge the chicken in the marinade, cover, and refrigerate for at least 1 hour or up to overnight. The longer it marinates, the more flavorful and juicier the chicken will be once fried.

2. In a large bowl, make the dredge by whisking together the flour, cornstarch, garlic powder, salt, smoked paprika, and cayenne, then set aside until you're ready to fry the chicken.

Bake the Biscuits:

3. In a large bowl, whisk together the flour, baking powder, sugar, salt, and baking soda. Using a box grater, shred the frozen butter directly into the flour mixture and gently toss to coat the butter pieces. Slowly pour in the buttermilk and mix with a wooden spoon or rubber spatula until just combined and a shaggy dough forms. The dough will look dry.

4. Turn the dough onto a clean surface and press it into a rough rectangle. Be sure to do this quickly and to not overwork the dough; you want the dough to stay as cold as possible. Using a rolling pin, roll the dough into roughly an 8 x 10-inch rectangle, then fold it into thirds like a trifolded letter. Turn the dough 90 degrees and roll it out again. Repeat the folding and rolling for a total of 4 or 5 folds. Use your hands to quickly form a rectangle, approximately 4½ x 8 inches and about 1 inch thick. Transfer the dough to the sheet tray and freeze for 30 minutes. This helps the butter stay cold and the biscuits to be flaky when baked.

5. Preheat the oven to 375°F and line a sheet tray with parchment paper. Once dough has chilled and rested, transfer the dough to a cutting board. Using a lightly floured knife, trim the edges and cut into 6 square biscuits. Transfer the dough squares to the lined sheet tray spaced about 2 inches apart. Brush the tops of each biscuit with melted butter. Bake until risen and golden brown, about 15 to 20 minutes. Remove from the oven and brush the warm biscuits with the honey and let cool on a wire rack, then cut in half for sandwiches.

Cook the Hot Maple Syrup:

6. In a small sauté pan, combine the maple syrup and sriracha. Cook over medium heat until just beginning to simmer. Keep warm until ready to use.

Fry the Chicken:

7. In a countertop fryer, heat the neutral oil over medium-high heat to 350°F. Remove the chicken from the marinade, letting excess liquid drip off. Toss the chicken in the dredge to coat completely, then carefully place it into the hot oil. Fry until golden brown and cooked through (with an internal temperature of 165°F). Remove the chicken to a wire rack set over a sheet tray and season lightly with salt.

Build the Sandwiches:

8. Start with the bottom half of the biscuit. Add a layer of pickles, followed by a piece of fried chicken. Drizzle with hot maple syrup, then top with the other half of the biscuit.

ALL THE WAYS TO
Cook AN Egg

We provide suggestions on the tastiest type of egg for each of the applicable morning sandwich recipes, but you can use any style you please—fried, over easy, scrambled, poached—they are, for the most part, interchangeable. We are here to guide you, but you are the master of your own universe. Here's a handy infographic to help you on your journey.

A. Sunny Side Up
B. Hard-Boiled
C. Poached
D. Omelet
E. Soft-Boiled
F. Fried
G. Scrambled
H. Baked

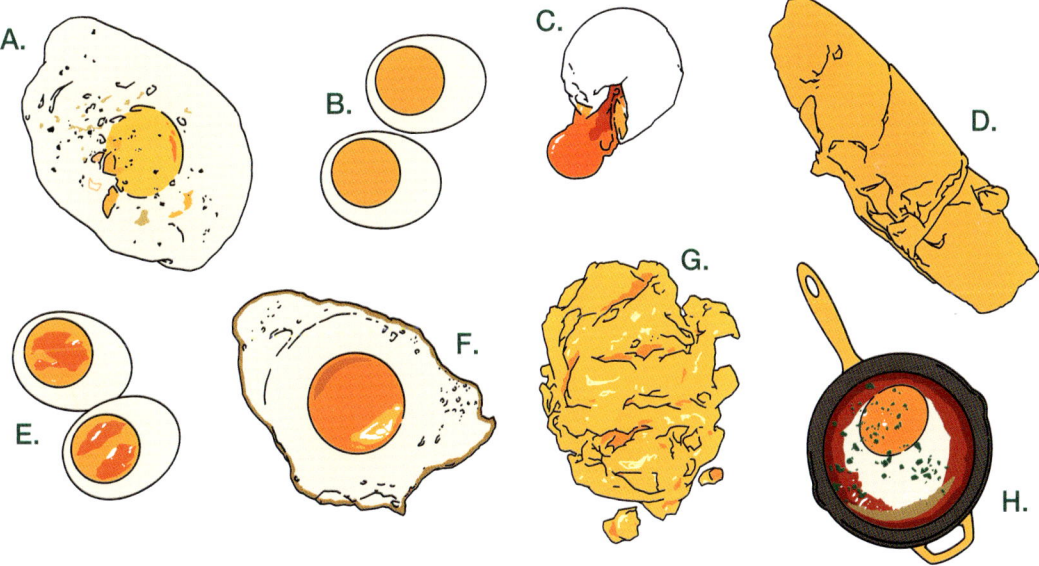

STEAK AND EGGS

Makes 2 sandwiches
Prep Time: 10 minutes
Cook Time: 20 minutes

Fun fact: Steak and eggs are the traditional pre-flight breakfast for NASA. The custom began in 1961 with Alan Shepard, the first American to go to space. And get this, the Aerospace Medical Laboratory chose this specific meal because it was "low residue," meaning it had a low fiber content and would result in fewer space poops. You should make this sandwich even if you aren't going to the moon. We added ground coffee to the dry rub to counteract the "low residue" effects. It also adds depth and flavor (which is the real reason why we did it). When you add the egg and sandwich it between two crusty pieces of ciabatta, well, you have a meal fit for both an astronaut *and* an idiot. We sh*t you not.

INGREDIENTS

Dry Rub:
1 teaspoon smoked paprika

2 teaspoons ground coffee

2 teaspoons ancho chile powder

Cowboy Steak:
12- to 16-ounce bone-in rib eye steak or boneless New York strip steak

2 tablespoons olive oil

1 large white onion, cut into thick slices

5 large garlic cloves, smashed

4 tablespoons unsalted butter

1 to 2 scallions, whites and greens separated (greens reserved for the eggs), sliced ¼ inch thick

Juice of 1 lime

Ciabatta:
4 tablespoons unsalted butter, softened

2 large garlic cloves, minced

1 large or 2 small pieces ciabatta

Eggs:
2 teaspoons olive oil

4 large eggs

2 tablespoons unsalted butter

Scallion greens from above

Sandwich Assembly:
2 tablespoons chopped fresh cilantro

Kosher salt

Ground black pepper

NOTES FOR THE IDIOTS

Remove the steak from the refrigerator 15 minutes before cooking to soften the fat cap.

continued

INSTRUCTIONS

Prepare the Dry Rub:

1. In a small bowl, combine the smoked paprika, ground coffee, and chile powder and set aside.

Cook the Cowboy Steak:

2. Heat a large cast-iron skillet over medium-high heat. Season the steak with the salt, then sprinkle the steak with the spice mixture on each side using one-quarter of the spice mixture. Press the spices into the steak as you season. Add the olive oil to the hot skillet, and when the oil is hot and shimmering gently, lay the steak in the center.

3. Add onions and smashed garlic into the pan around the steak as it cooks to begin to caramelize. Add the butter around the steak and onions and let it melt. Cook the steak until it forms a crust on the bottom, 3 to 4 minutes. Flip the steak and continue cooking, using the rendered fat to cook the onions and garlic.

4. Add the scallion whites to the skillet and continue cooking for another 3 to 4 minutes, until the steak reaches 130°F or your desired doneness. Squeeze the lime over the steak as it finishes cooking, then remove from the heat. Put the steak on a tray and pour the onions and pan juices over the steak. Let the steak rest for 5 minutes, then slice ¼ inch thick. Wipe the pan and place it over medium heat while you prepare the bread.

Toast the Ciabatta:

5. In a small bowl, combine the butter, garlic, and remaining dry rub. Cut the ciabatta in half and spread the butter mixture over the cut sides. Toast the bread in the pan cut side down until golden brown and crisp, about 3 minutes. Remove from the heat and set aside until ready to assemble.

Fry the Eggs:

6. Heat a large nonstick skillet over medium heat. Add 1 teaspoon of the olive oil and heat until the oil shimmers. Crack 2 eggs into the center of the pan. Season lightly with salt. Add 1 tablespoon of the butter to the skillet and let it melt. Sprinkle with half of the scallion greens. Use a spoon to baste the eggs until the whites are set and the yolk is jammy, about 3 minutes. Repeat with the remaining 2 eggs.

Build the Sandwiches:

7. Begin with the bottom half of the ciabatta. Add the steak slices, followed by the onions and two fried eggs. Garnish with cilantro, then add the ciabatta top.

BACON JAM AND CHILE EGG BISCUIT

Makes 6 sandwiches
Prep Time: 40 minutes
Cook Time: 1 hour

Nothing beats a biscuit in the morning, and this recipe, along with the Fried Chicken Biscuit (page 37), aims to please. Yes, biscuits take some extra work, and yes, they can be tough to pull off. (And we do mean tough—if you overmix them, they tend to take on the texture of concrete.) But never fear, because we've teed you up for success. First, you'll grate frozen butter into the dough to achieve perfect fat distribution. Then you'll put folds in the dough like it's a gosh-dang sheet of puff pastry. We like to call this "flake insurance." Congratulations, you're about to eat a homemade biscuit—there's absolutely no way to mess this up.

INGREDIENTS

Bacon Jam:
1 pound bacon, diced
½ cup diced yellow onion
4 medium garlic cloves, minced
1 tablespoon smooth Dijon mustard
1½ tablespoons Worcestershire sauce
½ cup maple syrup
2 tablespoons light brown sugar
¼ teaspoon chile flakes
Pinch of kosher salt
Pinch of ground black pepper

Biscuits:
3 cups all-purpose flour
1 tablespoon baking powder
1 tablespoon granulated sugar
1½ teaspoons kosher salt
1 teaspoon baking soda
¾ cup (1½ sticks) unsalted butter, frozen
1¼ cups buttermilk
4 tablespoons (½ stick) unsalted butter, melted

Chile Fried Eggs:
6 teaspoons olive oil, separated
6 teaspoons unsalted butter, separated
6 large eggs
Kosher salt
Ground black pepper
Red chile flakes

Sandwich Assembly:
1 cup baby arugula or baby spinach

INSTRUCTIONS

Make the Bacon Jam:

1. In a large skillet over medium heat, cook the bacon until the fat renders and the bacon just begins to get crispy, about 10 minutes. Drain all but 2 tablespoons of rendered fat from the bacon and add the onions. Cook until the onions are nicely caramelized, about 20 minutes. Stir in the garlic, mustard, Worcestershire sauce, maple syrup, brown sugar, chile flakes, salt, and pepper. Increase the heat to medium-high and bring the mixture up to a boil.

continued

2. Reduce the heat to medium and simmer until thick and jammy, about 45 minutes. Keep warm or cool and refrigerate in an airtight container for up to 1 week.

Make the Biscuits:

3. In a large bowl, whisk together the flour, baking powder, sugar, salt, and baking soda. Using a box grater, shred the frozen butter directly into the flour mixture and gently toss to coat the butter pieces.

4. Slowly pour in the buttermilk and mix with a wooden spoon or rubber spatula until just combined and a shaggy dough forms. The dough will look dry. Turn the dough onto a clean surface and press it into a rough rectangle. Be sure to do this quickly and to not overwork the dough—you want the dough to stay as cold as possible.

5. Using a rolling pin, roll the dough into roughly an 8 x 10-inch rectangle, then fold into thirds like a trifolded letter. Turn the dough 90 degrees and roll it out again. Repeat folding and rolling for a total of 4 or 5 folds. Use your hands to quickly form a rectangle about 4½ x 8 inches and about 1 inch thick. Transfer the dough to the sheet tray and freeze for 30 minutes. This helps the butter stay cold and the biscuits to be flaky when baked.

6. Preheat the oven to 375°F and line a sheet tray with parchment paper. Once dough has chilled and rested, transfer the dough to a cutting board; using a lightly floured knife, trim the edges and cut into 6 square biscuits. Transfer the dough squares to the lined sheet tray and space about 2 inches apart. Brush the tops of each biscuit with melted butter. Bake until risen and golden brown, about 15 to 20 minutes. Remove from the oven and cool on a wire rack, then cut in half for sandwiches.

Cook the Chile Fried Eggs:

7. Heat 1 teaspoon olive oil and 1 teaspoon butter in a small nonstick skillet over medium-high heat. Crack an egg into the skillet and cook until edges are slightly crisp, and the whites are set. Cover with lid, if needed, to finish cooking so the yolk stays runny when the whites are set. Season to taste with the salt, pepper, and red chile flakes, then remove from the pan. Repeat with the remaining eggs.

Build the Sandwiches:

8. Begin with the bottom half of the biscuit and spread with the bacon jam. Add a chile fried egg, followed by a layer of arugula. Finish with the top half of the biscuit.

NOTES FOR THE IDIOTS

Listen, are homemade biscuits almost always better than those store-bought kinds that you pop from a canister? Undeniably so. But sometimes we make sacrifices in life, and this could be one of them. If the toil of preparing biscuits from scratch makes your stomach sink, then by all means, support your local doughboy.

CHOPPED SAUSAGE SANDWICH

Makes 4 sandwiches
Prep Time: 15 minutes
Cook Time: 20 minutes

INGREDIENTS

Chopped Sausage:

2 tablespoons neutral oil

1 cup diced white onion

1 pound pork breakfast sausage

4 slices American cheese

4 slices provolone cheese

Scrambled Eggs:

8 large eggs

Sandwich Assembly:

2 Italian sesame hoagies, hinged and toasted

4 tablespoons mayonnaise

Spicy Ketchup (page 203)

Kosher salt

Ground black pepper

THE MORE YOU KNOW
(ABOUT SANDWICHES)

The first-ever six-foot sub is attributed to Manganaro's, an Italian food emporium on 9th Avenue in New York City in the 1950s. One foot wide and delivered on a custom board, it weighed 25 pounds, served 40 adults, and cost $28.50.

This is our ode to the bodegas of Harlem, New York City, a breakfast version of the classic chopped cheese. The exact origin of chopped cheese is up for debate, but most agree it was created in the 1990s at Hajji's Deli in Spanish Harlem, and it is exactly what it sounds like: meat, usually ground beef, chopped up with onions and American cheese as it cooks on a griddle. The cheese melts, and the beef and onions caramelize before it's slathered onto a hero roll. We did all that, but with sausage, and we added eggs, because breakfast.

INSTRUCTIONS

Make the Chopped Sausage:

1. Put the neutral oil and onion in a medium skillet or griddle over medium heat. Cook until tender and starting to caramelize, 5 to 10 minutes. Move the onions to the side of the pan and let them continue to cook. Add the sausage to the other side and let it caramelize, forming a crust on the edges, about 5 minutes. Chop the sausage into small pieces with the edge of your spatula. Mix the onions back into the sausage and continue to caramelize, chopping the meat as you go.

2. Once the sausage is fully cooked and caramelized, lay the slices of American and provolone cheese on top. Chop the cheese into the meat mixture a few times to combine. Season to taste with the salt and pepper. Remove the sausage mixture from the pan and reserve for assembly. Keep any rendered sausage fat in the pan and turn the heat down to low.

Scramble the Eggs:

3. In a medium bowl, whisk the eggs until the whites and yolks are fully combined. Pour the eggs into the pan with the remaining sausage fat.

4. Stir occasionally with a rubber spatula to cook them while keeping them in larger pieces, about 2 to 5 minutes. Season to taste with salt and pepper and reserve for assembly.

Build the Sandwiches:

5. Spread Spicy Ketchup on the bottom half of the Italian roll. Add the chopped sausage and scrambled eggs, then spread mayonnaise on the top half of the roll and close the sandwich.

TURKEY BREAKFAST CLUB

Makes 4 sandwiches
Prep Time: 20 minutes
Cook Time: 1 hour 30 minutes

INGREDIENTS

Herb Butter Turkey Breast:

½ cup (1 stick) unsalted butter, softened

1 tablespoon fresh thyme leaves, chopped

1 tablespoon chopped fresh rosemary

¼ cup chopped fresh parsley

1 teaspoon kosher salt, plus more to season the turkey

½ teaspoon ground black pepper, plus more to season the turkey

2 pounds turkey breast, skin on with rib

Chile Fried Eggs:

2 teaspoons olive oil, separated

2 teaspoons unsalted butter, separated

4 large eggs

Kosher salt

Ground black pepper

2 pinches of chile flakes

Sandwich Assembly:

2 large croissants, cut in half lengthwise and toasted

Basil Mayo (page 201)

1½ cups arugula

8 slices large heirloom tomato

8 slices Crispy Prosciutto (page 207), or substitute crispy bacon

Club sandwiches aren't generally considered breakfast food. But most club sandwiches don't come with a chile fried egg on a toasted croissant, either. One bite of this flaky, gooey concoction and you'll be begging for detention, or really any reason to get sent to the Breakfast Club.

INSTRUCTIONS

Roast the Turkey:

1. Preheat the oven to 400°F. In a small bowl, mix the softened butter with the thyme, rosemary, parsley, salt, and pepper. Season the turkey breast with salt and pepper, then rub with the herb butter both under the skin and on the outside. Place the turkey in a cast-iron or roasting pan and roast for 30 to 45 minutes, until the skin is browned and crispy.

2. Lower the oven temperature to 300°F and roast for an additional 15 to 30 minutes, until the internal temperature reaches 160°F. Cover with aluminum foil, if needed, to prevent overbrowning the turkey skin. Remove from the oven to a cutting board and let the turkey rest for at least 15 minutes, then cut into ¼-inch-thick slices. Let the slices marinate in the turkey drippings for added flavor. The turkey can be made ahead of time and stored in the refrigerator for up to 4 days. Warm when you're ready to use it.

Fry the Eggs:

3. In a small nonstick skillet, heat 1 teaspoon of the olive oil and 1 teaspoon of the butter. Once the butter is melted and bubbling, season with a pinch of salt and black pepper.

4. Crack 2 eggs into the skillet and cook until the edges are crispy and the whites are set, basting with the hot fat. Sprinkle with a pinch of chile flakes, then remove from the skillet. Repeat with the remaining eggs.

Build the Sandwiches:

5. Start with slathering both halves of your croissant with Basil Mayo. On the bottom half, add three to five slices of turkey, followed by two slices of prosciutto and two slices of tomato. Layer on a chile fried egg and arugula and finish with the top half of the croissant.

NOTES FOR THE IDIOTS

To cut an hour off the cook time, use deli sliced turkey meat instead of roasting the turkey breast from scratch.

PASTRAMI EGG AND CHEESE

Makes 4 sandwiches
Prep Time: 15 minutes
Cook Time: 15 minutes

INGREDIENTS

Scrambled Eggs:

4 tablespoons unsalted butter

8 large eggs

2 tablespoons whole grain mustard

¼ cup crème fraîche

2 tablespoons chopped fresh chives

Kosher salt

Ground black pepper

Sandwich Assembly:

4 tablespoons softened unsalted butter

8 slices pretzel bread

2 tablespoons whole grain mustard

Red Wine Cabbage (page 215), warmed

8 slices Swiss cheese

1 pound pastrami, sliced

Horseradish Cream Cheese (page 196)

Most days, heaping piles of pastrami are relegated to afternoon, evening, or even late-night fare, but we say no more. Pastrami can be a breakfast food, too. Slice it any way you like, thick or thin. Just promise you'll make it soon and don't save it for a special occasion, because making it IS the special occasion

INSTRUCTIONS

Scramble the Eggs:

1. Preheat a medium nonstick sauté pan over medium-low heat with 2 tablespoons of the butter. Crack the eggs into a medium bowl and whisk until the yolks and whites are combined. Once the butter is melted, pour the whisked eggs into the pan.

2. Stir frequently with a rubber spatula, pushing the eggs around gently as the eggs begin to set. Add the mustard and crème fraîche and stir in the remaining 2 tablespoons of butter, incorporating all the ingredients into the eggs. The scrambled eggs should be soft, creamy, and fluffy. Finish the eggs by folding in the chives. Remove the eggs from the pan and wipe out the pan.

Cook and Build the Sandwiches:

3. Build your sandwich by spreading a thin layer of softened butter on the pretzel bread. Flip your slices and spread mustard on half of the slices and Horseradish Cream Cheese on the other halves. Top the mustard halves with a heaping amount of warm Red Wine Cabbage, scrambled eggs, and 2 slices of cheese. Top with the Horseradish Cream Cheese halves and gently press the two halves together.

4. Place the nonstick pan back on the stove over medium heat. Add the assembled sandwiches, two at a time, and toast each side for about 90 seconds, or until golden brown.

NOON

Ah yes, noon sandwiches. This is the idiot's time to shine, for the middle of the day is clearly the best time to eat a sandwich. Daydreaming of a Reuben so high it touches the sky (page 66) will help anyone get through a morning meeting. And nothing goes better with a secret pint at lunch than a crispy beer-battered fish sandwich (page 99). (This is actually a double win, because you can blame your breath on the batter when you get back to work—not today, HR! Not today.)

If we're being honest, and we always are, pretty much any sandwich can be a *Noon Sandwich*, but we did draw some boundaries for the sake of the organization of this book. The sandwiches in this chapter are a little easier to make, or at the very least, they can be made more quickly, and they aren't overly heavy, so you can continue on with your day in style. Well, except for the pork belly one (page 55). You're gonna want to sleep that one off. Lucky for you, afternoon naps are just as glorious as an afternoon sandwich.

Pork Belly   55

Chinese Chicken Salad   56

Susi Vidal's Spicy Chicken Parm   59

Curried Chickpea Salad   62

Bologna and Cheese, Baby!   65

Sky High Reuben   66

Emmanuel Duverneau's Caprese Chicken   69

Spanish Prawns   70

Fried Green BLT Sliders   73

H Woo's Thai Fried Chicken   75

Chip Butty   79

Egg Salad, Japanese Style   81

Summer Squash Sandwich   83

Nik Barricelli's Sicilian Steak Sandwich   85

Herbaceous Crab Salad   89

Zach King's Steak Bánh Mì   91

Onigirazu: A Japanese Sushi Sandwich   93

Falafel Pita   95

Fish, No Chips   99

Matt Stonie's Mississippi Shrimp Slugburger   101

Pastrami Salmon   103

PORK BELLY

Makes 4 sandwiches
Prep Time: 20 minutes
Cook Time: 40 minutes

INGREDIENTS

Hot Honey:

1 cup honey

1 tablespoon hot sauce

2 tablespoons red chile flakes

Pork Belly:

2 teaspoons dark chili powder

1 tablespoon packed brown sugar

1 teaspoon smoked paprika

1 teaspoon garlic powder

1 teaspoon onion powder

¼ teaspoon cayenne pepper

1 teaspoon kosher salt

¼ teaspoon ground black pepper

1 pound pork belly, skin removed, cut into ¾-inch slices (about 8 pieces)

Sandwich Assembly:

4 sesame kaiser rolls, cut in half lengthwise, toasted

Whole Grain Mustard Mayo (page 202)

Corn Relish (page 215)

8 slices from 2 large tomatoes (¼ inch thick)

4 romaine lettuce leaves, torn to fit the buns

Pork belly is a lot like a long-lost, unrequited love. Partaking in it often is probably a bad idea, but a little taste every now and then, and . . . well . . . what could possibly go wrong? We added some pickled corn relish to cut through all the fattiness. Think of it as the therapy session that immediately follows your tryst; a way to make amends, if not with your ex, then at least with yourself.

INSTRUCTIONS

Prepare the Hot Honey:

1. In a small saucepan, combine the honey, hot sauce, and chile flakes. Stir over medium heat until the honey reaches a simmer, then remove from the heat. Let the honey continue to infuse with the chile flakes as it cools completely.

2. Strain out the chile flakes and store the hot honey in an airtight container in a cool, dry place for up to 1 month.

Roast the Pork Belly:

3. Preheat the oven to 400°F and line a sheet tray with parchment paper. In a medium bowl, mix the chili powder, brown sugar, paprika, garlic powder, onion powder, cayenne, salt, and pepper. Add the sliced pork belly and toss with the spice mixture to coat evenly. Place the seasoned pork belly on the prepared sheet tray.

4. Bake for about 20 minutes, until caramelized on top. Remove from the oven, flip all the pieces, and continue baking for another 20 minutes, or until caramelized all over and tender. Brush with hot honey and return to the oven until the honey caramelizes, another 15 to 20 minutes.

Build the Sandwiches:

5. Start with slathering both halves of your kaiser roll with Whole Grain Mustard Mayo. Starting from the bottom, layer on romaine lettuce, two slices of tomato, and two slices of pork belly. Add a heaping spoonful of Corn Relish, then drizzle with hot honey and finish with the kaiser roll top.

CHINESE CHICKEN SALAD

Makes 4 sandwiches
Prep Time: 30 minutes

Chinese chicken salad might be the original fusion food, originating in the 1960s among the Hollywood set. (They *do* love their salads in California, and now that we mention it, they love their fusion cuisine, too.) We don't stray too far from the original concept, other than turning it into a sandwich, cause that's what we do best. You can make most of the components in advance, and use a store-bought rotisserie chicken, or even last night's leftovers, making this a super easy sandwich to prepare on the fly.

INGREDIENTS

Five-Spice Chicken Spread:

1 cup Japanese mayonnaise, such as Kewpie

3 tablespoons hoisin sauce

2 teaspoons Chinese five-spice powder

3 scallions, thinly sliced

1 pound roasted chicken, shredded and skin removed

Honey Mustard Slaw:

½ cup rice wine vinegar

¼ cup Dijon mustard

⅓ cup soy sauce

2 tablespoons honey

2 tablespoons chopped pickled ginger

¾ cup neutral oil

2 teaspoons toasted sesame oil

Pinch of red chile flakes

3 cups thinly sliced napa cabbage

½ cup julienned carrots

½ bunch scallions, thinly sliced

One 15-ounce can mandarin orange segments, drained

⅓ cup cashews, toasted

Sandwich Assembly:

Two 8- to 10-inch baguettes, cut in half lengthwise

¼ cup picked cilantro sprigs

Crispy Wontons (page 207)

Kosher salt

Ground black pepper

INSTRUCTIONS

Prepare the Five-Spice Chicken Spread:

1. In a small bowl, mix the mayonnaise, hoisin sauce, five-spice powder, and chopped scallions. Season to taste with salt and pepper.

2. In a medium bowl, combine the shredded chicken with ¾ cup of the five-spice spread. If the chicken mixture seems dry, gradually add more five-spice spread until you reach your desired consistency. Adjust seasoning as needed with salt and pepper. Set aside or refrigerate for up to 2 days, until ready for assembly.

Make the Honey Mustard Slaw:

3. In a medium bowl, combine the vinegar, mustard, soy sauce, honey, and pickled ginger. Slowly drizzle in the neutral oil and then the sesame oil while whisking. Season with a pinch of salt, pepper, and chile flakes.

4. In a large bowl, combine the cabbage, carrots, scallions, mandarin orange segments, and cashews. Add the dressing, toss to combine, and adjust the salt to taste.

Build the Sandwiches:

5. Start by spreading five-spice spread on both halves of your baguette. On the bottom half, layer five-spice chicken salad, followed by honey mustard slaw, crispy wontons, and a sprinkle of cilantro. Top with the other half of the baguette.

SUSI VIDAL'S SPICY CHICKEN PARM

Makes 2 sandwiches
Prep Time: 30 minutes
Cook Time: 35 minutes

Call us crazy, but the only thing better than a chicken parm is a chicken parm sandwich. We know it, you know it, and Susi Vidal knows it. Susi, who has amassed quite a following on TikTok with her hilarious "Only Pans" account, made one when she graced the *Idiot Sandwich* stage—and it's been gracing our dreams ever since, so much so that we put a version of it in this book.

INGREDIENTS

Blistered Cherry Tomatoes:
1 tablespoon extra-virgin olive oil
8 to 10 cherry tomatoes

Parmesan Chicken:
1 to 2 cups neutral oil
1 cup all-purpose flour
2 large eggs, whisked
1 cup panko breadcrumbs
¾ cup shredded Parmesan cheese
2 tablespoons picked parsley leaves, minced
Two 6-ounce chicken breasts, pounded lightly to even thickness, patted dry
4 slices fresh mozzarella cheese

Arugula Salad:
1 cup (2 ounces) packed arugula
3 thin round slices of a small red onion
3 tablespoons shredded Parmesan cheese
Blistered cherry tomatoes
Extra-virgin olive oil
Fresh lemon juice

Sandwich Assembly:
2 ciabatta buns, sliced in half lengthwise and toasted
Pesto (page 199)
Kosher salt
Ground black pepper

NOTES FOR THE IDIOTS

To lighten the load, substitute store-bought sun-dried tomatoes for the blistered cherry tomatoes.
Susi Vidal might protest, but feel free to substitute store-bought pesto instead of making it from scratch.

continued

INSTRUCTIONS

Prepare the Blistered Cherry Tomatoes:

1. Heat the olive oil in a large skillet over high heat. Once the oil shimmers, add the cherry tomatoes, season with a pinch of salt and pepper, and toss. Let the tomatoes sit in the pan to caramelize, shaking the pan occasionally, for 5 to 10 minutes, until they burst, are softened, and begin to caramelize lightly. Remove from the pan and set aside to cool. Wipe the pan.

Cook the Parmesan Chicken:

2. Add 1 to 2 cups of neutral oil to the skillet, until there is about an inch of oil in the bottom of the pan. Heat over medium heat until it reaches 350°F. Meanwhile, preheat the broiler to high.
3. Set up three shallow bowls: Bowl 1: Dump in the all-purpose flour. Bowl 2: Whisk the eggs. Bowl 3: Combine the panko, Parmesan cheese, and parsley.
4. Season the chicken breasts with the salt and pepper. Dredge the chicken in the flour, shaking off any excess. Dip the chicken into the whisked eggs to coat completely, then press into the panko mixture.
5. Carefully add the breaded chicken to the oil and cook until crispy and golden brown, about 5 minutes, then flip and cook the other side. Continue to cook until the breading is evenly golden brown and the internal temperature reaches 165°F. Remove the chicken from the oil and let it rest on a wire rack set over a sheet tray. Place the chicken in the skillet used for the cherry tomatoes and top each piece with a slice of mozzarella cheese. Place under the broiler and broil until the cheese is melted, caramelized, and bubbling, about 4 minutes.

Prepare the Arugula Salad:

6. In a large bowl, combine the arugula, onion, Parmesan cheese, and blistered cherry tomatoes. Season with a pinch of salt and pepper and lightly drizzle with olive oil and lemon juice.

Build the Sandwiches:

7. Spread Pesto on both halves of the ciabatta. On the bottom half, add the Parmesan chicken, then top with the arugula salad. Finish with the top half of the ciabatta.

THE EARL OF SANDWICH
MAN, MYTH, AND LEGEND

You can find all of this information on Wikipedia, but we thought we'd save you some googling and provide everything you need to know about our man Earl right here, starting with the fact that his name is not Earl. He lived hard, he lived fast, and his name was John Montagu, the 4th Earl of Sandwich. He was a compulsive gambler who couldn't possibly step away from the table, so he had his valet bring him salt beef stuffed between two slices of toast. He had traveled to the Ottoman Empire as a young man, which is most likely where he got the idea. Everyone called it a sandwich, and we like to believe it was because the word *ottoman* had already been taken to describe furniture.

We aren't ones to libel, so we should tell you that some historians think his questionable reputation was unfounded—that it wasn't a gambling table he couldn't step away from but his desk. He was highly involved in the military and politics, and his work ethic could be summed up by this popular saying about him: "Seldom has any man held so many offices and accomplished so little." He had one child with his wife, and when her physical and mental health began to decline, he went on to have somewhere between five and nine children with his mistress (the exact number is up for debate). He was allegedly in the Hellfire Club, which was quite scandalous. (You will need to google that one, because we are running out of space.) RIP, Earl of Sandwich. We hardly knew ye, but we sure do love your namesake.

CURRIED CHICKPEA SALAD

Makes 2 sandwiches
Prep Time: 20 minutes

This one's for all you health nuts. Chickpeas are high in "iums"—calcium, magnesium, potassium, and selenium. They are also stacked with fiber, vitamin B, and iron. But health is only half the picture. Here, we have one of the few Venn diagrams where "really good for you" and "exceptionally tasty" actually overlap. Don't take this recipe for granted, she's a chickpea in a sea of lima beans.

INGREDIENTS

Raita:

½ cup plain Greek yogurt

1 teaspoon honey

¼ cup seeded and diced English or Persian cucumber

2 tablespoons finely chopped red onion

1 tablespoon chopped fresh cilantro

¼ teaspoon ground cumin

¼ teaspoon kosher salt, plus more to taste

1 teaspoon minced Fresno chile, optional

Curried Chickpea Salad:

One 15-ounce can chickpeas, drained and rinsed

2 tablespoons finely diced red onion

2 tablespoons finely diced celery

2 tablespoons thinly sliced scallion

Juice of 1 large lime

1 tablespoon chopped fresh cilantro

1 tablespoon Dijon or whole grain mustard

⅓ cup mayonnaise

1 tablespoon curry powder

½ cup julienned or chopped Pickled Apricot (page 213)

Sandwich Assembly:

1 pita bread, cut in half and each half opened to form a pocket

½ small green apple, cored and thinly sliced into half moons

½ cup alfalfa sprouts, or substitute with another sprout or green of choice

8 mint leaves, picked

12 cilantro leaves, picked

INSTRUCTIONS

Prepare the Raita:

1. In a small bowl, whisk the honey into the yogurt. Add the cucumbers, red onion, cilantro, cumin, salt, and chile, if using, and mix together thoroughly. Season with additional salt to taste. Chill in the refrigerator until ready to assemble.

Make the Curried Chickpeas:

2. In a medium bowl, mash one-third of the chickpeas with a fork until you achieve a chunky puree texture. Fold in the remaining chickpeas, the red onion, celery, scallion, lime juice, mustard, mayonnaise, curry powder, and Pickled Apricots and mix until well combined. Season with the salt.

Build the Sandwiches:

3. Fill the pita pocket with Curried Chickpea Salad. Add four to six slices of green apple, alfalfa sprouts, mint, and cilantro leaves. Serve with the raita.

NOTES FOR THE IDIOTS

Storing the potato slices in ice water in the fridge for at least 30 minutes removes excess starch and results in a crispier chip.

BOLOGNA AND CHEESE, BABY!

Makes 4 sandwiches
Prep Time: 30 minutes
Cook Time: 20 minutes

This is your childhood fantasy sandwich dream come true because it has all the components of a basic bologna and cheese, but majorly super-heroed up. The bologna is fried. The cheese—pimiento. We even threw some homemade potato chips in the mix. Little you would be so proud of the idiot you became.

INGREDIENTS

Pimiento Cheese:
or substitute with store-bought

1 cup extra-sharp cheddar cheese, shredded

4 ounces cream cheese, softened

2 ounces jarred pimientos, drained and chopped

1 tablespoon mayonnaise, plus more, if needed

¼ teaspoon garlic powder

¼ teaspoon onion powder

¼ teaspoon cayenne pepper

¼ teaspoon smoked paprika

3 tablespoons thinly sliced scallions

Homemade Potato Chips:
1 quart neutral oil, for frying

1 russet potato, thinly sliced lengthwise on a mandoline

Kosher salt

Bologna:
2 tablespoons neutral oil

16 slices bologna, at least ⅛ inch thick

Sandwich Assembly:
8 slices white bread, toasted

Yellow mustard

2 cups shredded iceberg lettuce (½ small head)

INSTRUCTIONS

Make the Pimiento Cheese:

1. In a medium bowl, combine the cheeses, pimientos, mayonnaise, garlic powder, onion powder, cayenne, smoked paprika, and scallions evenly using a rubber spatula. Chill for 30 minutes to allow the flavors to meld. Adjust the thickness with additional mayonnaise, if needed, to desired consistency.

Make the Potato Chips:

2. Thinly slice the potato lengthwise on a mandoline and place the slices in a bowl of ice water. Let soak for at least 30 minutes.

3. In a countertop fryer or large pot, heat the neutral oil over medium-high heat to 350°F. Remove the potato slices from the water and pat them dry in a single layer to remove excess water.

4. Add the potato slices to the hot oil and fry, rotating frequently, for about 5 minutes, until crisp and evenly golden brown. Remove the chips onto a tray or plate lined with paper towels and sprinkle with salt.

5. Repeat with the remaining potato slices. Set aside for assembly.

Cook the Bologna:

6. Heat the neutral oil in a large skillet over medium heat. Add the bologna slices and cook for 1½ minutes on each side, or until golden brown and caramelized.

Build the Sandwiches:

7. On a slice of toasted white bread, add a layer of pimiento cheese, followed by iceberg lettuce, four slices of bologna, and potato chips. Top with the second slice of white bread and spread with a generous amount of mustard.

SKY HIGH REUBEN

Makes 2 sandwiches
Prep Time: 15 minutes
Cook Time: 15 minutes

INGREDIENTS

Thousand Island Dressing:

½ cup mayonnaise

¼ cup ketchup

¼ cup minced dill pickle

2 tablespoons prepared horseradish

Juice of 1 lemon

Kosher salt

Sauerkraut and Corned Beef:

4 tablespoons (½ stick) unsalted butter

¾ cup good-quality sauerkraut, drained and squeezed

Pinch of ground black pepper

1 pound cooked corned beef, sliced

Sandwich Assembly:

6 slices good-quality Swiss or Gruyère cheese

4 slices rye bread

If the Tower of Babel were a sandwich, it would be this one. Not because our Reuben is a symbol of mankind's ego, not even because we stack it as high as the heavens, but simply because, as we were developing it, all the recipe testers blacked out for a second and awoke speaking completely different languages.* Maybe that's why some of the cheese ended up on the outside of the sandwich, instead of inside where it belongs. At any rate, it's a miracle we finished. Plus, it's so big, it could feed a small village, which is also kind of a miracle.

*We're just goofing! No recipe testers were harmed in the making of this sandwich.

INSTRUCTIONS

Make the Thousand Island Dressing:

1. In a small bowl, combine the mayonnaise, ketchup, minced dill pickle, horseradish, and lemon juice. Whisk to combine, season with salt, then reserve for assembly.

Cook the Sauerkraut:

2. In a large nonstick skillet, melt 2 tablespoons of the butter over high heat. Add the drained and squeezed sauerkraut. Cook for about 5 minutes, until lightly caramelized, then season with pepper. Wipe the skillet clean.

Cook the Corned Beef:

3. Return the skillet to medium-high heat and melt the remaining 2 tablespoons butter. Add the corned beef and cook until it begins to crisp on both sides, about 1½ minutes on each side. Remove the corned beef and set aside for assembly. Wipe the pan and return to the stovetop for cooking the sandwiches.

Cook the Sandwiches:

4. Turn the burner under the skillet to medium. Place 2 slices of Swiss cheese on the skillet. Top each cheese slice with a slice of bread and cook until the cheese melts and adheres to the bread, creating a cheese crust.
5. Put another slice of cheese on top of one bread slice and let it melt. Pile a generous amount of sauerkraut on top of this slice. Spread the dressing on the other slice of the bread and top with the crispy corned beef.
6. Cook until the cheese on the face-down side of the bread is golden, then remove from the skillet and sandwich the two halves together with the crusted cheese on the outside.

THE MORE YOU KNOW
(ABOUT SANDWICHES)

The world's largest sandwich weighed 5,440 pounds. It was made in Roseville, Michigan, in 2005, was 12 feet long, and was filled with corned beef, lettuce, cheese, and mustard.

EMMANUEL DUVERNEAU'S CAPRESE CHICKEN

Makes 4 sandwiches
Prep Time: 20 minutes
Cook Time: 15 minutes

When Emmanuel Duverneau won the *Idiot Sandwich* competition, he slid right off the screen and into our hearts. At first, we weren't sure if his caprese chicken could measure up to his famous dance moves, but boy did he prove us wrong. One bite, with its thinly pounded chicken breast, basil aioli, and hodgepodge of other toppings, and we were hooked. Thanks for showing us your moves, Manny.

INGREDIENTS

Basil Aioli:

5 small garlic cloves

1 cup mayonnaise

1 tablespoon lemon zest

1 tablespoon fresh lemon juice

1¼ cups packed fresh basil leaves

1 teaspoon kosher salt

Chicken Breasts:

1 tablespoon olive oil

Two 8-ounce chicken breasts, cut in half lengthwise and pounded to ¼ inch thickness

2½ teaspoons kosher salt

¼ teaspoon ground black pepper

⅛ teaspoon garlic powder

Sandwich Assembly:

1 Italian loaf, cut in half lengthwise

Balsamic glaze

½ cup sliced banana peppers

8 slices Crispy Prosciutto (page 207)

5 or 6 slices fresh mozzarella cheese

½ red onion, sliced into ¼-inch rounds

Six ½-inch-thick slices beefsteak tomato

½ cup shredded iceberg lettuce

INSTRUCTIONS

Make the Basil Aioli:

1. In a food processor, combine the garlic, mayonnaise, and lemon zest and juice. Process to combine thoroughly, scraping the bowl with a rubber spatula as needed. Add the basil and salt and process until the aioli is green and the basil is well chopped. Adjust seasoning to taste and set aside and reserve for assembly.

Sear the Chicken Breasts:

2. Heat a large skillet over medium-high heat and add the olive oil. Season the chicken with the salt, pepper, and garlic powder.

3. Once the oil is shimmering, sear the chicken for 3 to 5 minutes per side, until browned and the internal temperature reaches 165°F.

Build the Sandwiches:

4. Spread basil aioli on both halves of the Italian loaf. Starting with the bottom half of the loaf, layer on iceberg lettuce, tomatoes, red onion, and chicken breast. Add fresh mozzarella, prosciutto, and banana peppers and drizzle with balsamic glaze. Top with the Italian loaf top and cut the loaf into 4 sandwiches.

SPANISH PRAWNS

Makes 4 sandwiches
Prep Time: 15 minutes
Cook Time: 20 minutes

This bad boy combines the traditional Spanish tapa of gambas al ajillo with pan-fried chorizo, tomatoes, and way too much garlic (as if there is such a thing). The result is nothing short of spectacular—a buttered baguette soaked in garlicky tomato sauce with the firm bite of juicy prawns and crispy pan-fried chorizo. Assuming you aren't a vampire, you are gonna love this freaking sandwich. Oh, and if you can't find prawns, just use shrimp. They are slightly smaller, but they'll do the trick.

INGREDIENTS

Prawns:

2 tablespoons extra-virgin olive oil

1 pound size 16/20 prawns (or shrimp), peeled and deveined with tails removed, patted dry

1 tablespoon fresh lemon juice

Chorizo Tomato Sauce:

8 ounces Spanish raw chorizo, casing removed, or substitute with Mexican chorizo

2 tablespoons extra-virgin olive oil, plus more as needed

3 tablespoons finely diced sweet onions

3 cups cherry tomatoes

1 tablespoon tomato paste

2 teaspoons paprika

1 teaspoon red chile flakes

1 cup vegetable stock

8 garlic cloves, thinly sliced

¼ cup green olives, pitted and halved

3 tablespoons chopped fresh parsley leaves

1 tablespoon fresh lemon juice

2 tablespoons unsalted butter

Pinch of kosher salt

Pinch of ground black pepper

Sandwich Assembly:

Two 8-inch baguettes, cut through so they are hinged, lightly toasted

Crispy Garlic (page 210)

Zest of ½ lemon

1 tablespoon chopped fresh parsley leaves

INSTRUCTIONS

Cook the Prawns:

1. In a large sauté pan, heat 1 tablespoon of the olive oil over medium-high heat. Once the oil is shimmering, add the prawns and cook for about 3 minutes, turning them midway, just until they turn pink.
2. Add the lemon juice, then remove the prawns from the pan and set aside. Return the pan to the stovetop.

Make the Chorizo Tomato Sauce:

3. To the pan, add the remaining tablespoon of oil then the chorizo and onions. Use a wooden spoon to break up the chorizo and cook until it's crispy and the onions are beginning to caramelize, about 5 minutes.
4. Add the cherry tomatoes and cook until they begin to burst, break down, and soften, about 3 minutes. Stir in the tomato paste, paprika, and chile flakes and continue to cook for 1 to 2 minutes. Add vegetable stock and garlic; lower the heat to medium-low, bring to a simmer, and continue cooking until the sauce thickens to a marinara consistency, 10 to 15 minutes.
5. Stir in the olives, parsley, lemon juice, and butter and season with the salt and pepper. Add the cooked prawns to the sauce to warm through.

Build the Sandwiches:

6. Start at the bottom half of the baguette and layer with chorizo tomato sauce. Add prawns, then sprinkle with parsley and lemon zest. Top with Crispy Garlic and close the baguette top.

FRIED GREEN BLT SLIDERS

Makes 6 sliders
Prep Time: 35 minutes
Cook Time: 20 minutes

The only thing that could possibly beat a classic BLT is a BLT with fried green tomatoes. It's so good, in fact, that it'll have you screaming "Towanda!" after the first bite. You may be wondering what "Towanda" is. Well, no spoilers, but it is a reference to the 1991 hit film *Fried Green Tomatoes*, starring Kathy Bates and Jessica Tandy. Let's just say it features some extra delicious BBQ sandwiches, and every idiot should see it at least once. When shopping for ingredients, be sure to get unripe tomatoes—they are firmer, and that's the key to them holding shape while frying.

P.S. We added some hot honey to the bacon, too, because of course we did. *Towanda!!!!*

INGREDIENTS

Spicy Remoulade:

½ cup mayonnaise

1 tablespoon whole grain or Dijon mustard

1 medium garlic clove, minced

1 tablespoon minced dill pickle

2 teaspoons fresh lemon juice

2 teaspoons minced fresh parsley

1 teaspoon Worcestershire sauce

1 tablespoon hot sauce

1 teaspoon paprika

½ teaspoon kosher salt, plus more to taste

Fried Green Tomatoes:

About 1 cup canola oil, for frying

Six ½-inch slices green tomatoes, about the size of your slider buns (about 2 green tomatoes)

½ cup all-purpose flour

1 teaspoon kosher salt

½ teaspoon ground black pepper

½ teaspoon smoked paprika

2 large eggs, beaten

½ cup buttermilk

½ cup cornmeal

1 tablespoon Cajun seasoning

Sandwich Assembly:

6 brioche slider buns, halved lengthwise and toasted

6 slices Hot Honey Bacon (page 206), cut in half to fit the buns

3 romaine lettuce leaves, torn to fit the size of your buns

continued

INSTRUCTIONS

Make the Spicy Remoulade:

1. In a small bowl, mix the mayonnaise, mustard, garlic, pickle, lemon juice, parsley, Worcestershire sauce, hot sauce, paprika, and salt. Adjust the salt to taste. Set aside for later.

Prep and Fry the Fried Green Tomatoes:

2. In a countertop fryer or large pot, heat 2 inches of neutral oil over medium-high heat to 375°F.
3. Prepare three shallow dishes: Dish 1: Mix the flour, salt, pepper, and paprika. Dish 2: Whisk the eggs and buttermilk. Dish 3: Dump in the cornmeal and mix in the Cajun seasoning.
4. Dip the green tomato slices into the seasoned flour, then into the egg mixture, and finally coat with the cornmeal, pressing down to ensure it sticks. For better coverage and to help the cornmeal mixture cling to the tomatoes, repeat the egg and cornmeal process.
5. Add the tomatoes to the hot oil and fry for 2 to 3 minutes per side, until golden brown and crispy. Drain on paper towels or a wire rack.

Build the Sandwiches:

6. Begin by slathering both halves of the slider buns with spicy remoulade. Starting on the bottom half of your slider bun, add a layer of romaine lettuce, followed by a fried green tomato slice and two pieces of Hot Honey Bacon. Finish with the top of the slider bun.

H WOO'S THAI FRIED CHICKEN

Makes 4 sandwiches
Prep Time: 30 minutes
Cook Time: 15 minutes

When H Woo Lee, founder of the *Maru Los Angeles* supper club–turned–TikTok sensation, competed on *Idiot Sandwich*, he had us hooked at the mention of *tempura fried chicken thighs*. Add a bright papaya salad and a Thai-style marinade to the mix, and of course he took home the prize. Consider yourself *wooed*.

INGREDIENTS

Thai Chicken:

6 bird's-eye chiles

1 stalk fresh lemongrass, minced (1 tablespoon), or use lemongrass paste

3 large garlic cloves, chopped

1½ teaspoons kosher salt

½ teaspoon ground black pepper

1 cup water

4 boneless, skinless chicken thighs

2 quarts neutral oil, for frying

Papaya Salad:

2 tablespoons coconut palm sugar or granulated sugar

1 large garlic clove

2 bird's-eye chiles

¼ cup fish sauce

¼ cup lime juice

1½ cups julienned unripe green papaya (julienne on a mandoline or by hand)

½ cup shredded carrot

1 jalapeño chile, thinly sliced, optional for additional heat

Tempura Batter:
or substitute with store-bought boxed tempura batter mix

1¼ cups tempura flour

⅓ cup tapioca flour

⅓ cup rice flour

1 teaspoon kosher salt

1 teaspoon ground black pepper

1½ cups ice-cold club soda

½ cup vodka, chilled, or substitute club soda

Sandwich Assembly:

4 brioche buns, halved lengthwise and toasted

Kewpie mayonnaise

Picked cilantro leaves

2 Roma tomatoes, sliced ¼ inch thick

continued

INSTRUCTIONS

Make the Thai Chicken Marinade:

1. Use a mortar and pestle to grind the chiles, lemongrass, garlic, salt, and pepper until a paste forms. Add the water and whisk to combine. Pour the marinade over the chicken, in a zip-top bag or covered bowl and refrigerate for at least 30 minutes or overnight.

Make the Papaya Salad:

2. In a mortar and pestle, make the dressing by grinding together the sugar, garlic, and bird's-eye chiles. Add the fish sauce and lime juice and mix to combine.
3. In a small bowl, add the papaya and carrots and toss with the dressing to coat completely. Add the jalapeño chile, if using. Set aside in the refrigerator until ready for assembly.

Cook the Tempura Chicken:

4. In a countertop fryer or large pot, heat the neutral oil over medium-high heat to 350°F. In a large bowl, make your tempura batter by combining the tempura flour, tapioca flour, rice flour, salt, and white pepper. Gently whisk in club soda and vodka, if using, until a batter forms.
5. Remove the chicken from the marinade and pat dry with paper towels. Dip the chicken into the tempura batter to coat completely. Carefully place the chicken in the hot oil and cook until the batter is crisp, and the internal temperature reaches 165°F, about 8 minutes. Remove the chicken and place it on a wire rack set over a sheet tray to drain excess oil.

Build the Sandwiches:

6. Start by spreading Kewpie mayonnaise on both halves of your bun. Add 1 to 2 slices of tomato, followed by tempura crispy chicken and a heaping amount of papaya salad. Sprinkle with cilantro and finish with the top of the brioche bun.

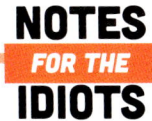

NOTES FOR THE IDIOTS

If you don't own a mortar and pestle, use a food processor. And if you don't own a food processor, chop it by hand.

Vodka makes tempura batter extra crispy because it evaporates faster than water and doesn't form as much gluten, leaving you with a lighter, crunchier coating.

CHIP BUTTY

Makes 2 sandwiches
Prep Time: 1 hour
Cook Time: 45 minutes

INGREDIENTS

Chips:

3 tablespoons kosher salt, plus more to taste

½ cup malt vinegar

1 pound Kennebec or russet potatoes, peeled and cut into batons (4 inches long and 1½ inches thick)

2 tablespoons neutral oil

Garlic Herb Butter:

½ cup (1 stick) unsalted butter, softened

2 medium garlic cloves, minced

2 tablespoons finely chopped fresh parsley

1 teaspoon kosher salt

½ teaspoon ground black pepper

Sandwich Assembly:

4 slices white bread

Spicy Ketchup, optional (page 203), or substitute with regular ketchup

We've said it once, and we'll say it again. The Brits get a bad rap when it comes to food (quite fairly, we might add). But—all demerits of Spotted Dick aside, they do have some really tasty inventions. The chip butty is one of them. We promise. For some reason it really pisses the Americans off, though. Something about the carb-on-carb action being completely unhinged. But, it's comfort food at its best, and it's also a nostalgia thing, okay?!

INSTRUCTIONS

Make the Chips:

1. In a large pot, bring 3 quarts of water with the salt and vinegar to a boil. Cook the potatoes in the water until just tender, about 6 minutes, being careful not to overcook them. Place the cooked potatoes on a wire rack to cool completely, then transfer to the freezer until firm, about 45 minutes.

2. Preheat the oven to 475°F. Remove the potatoes from the freezer and coat them completely in the oil. Arrange the potatoes in a single layer on a sheet tray. Roast until golden and crispy, about 20 minutes, then flip and cook for an additional 15 minutes. Season with additional salt to taste.

Make the Garlic Herb Butter:

3. In a small bowl, mix the butter, garlic, parsley, salt, and pepper to incorporate the ingredients.

Build the Sandwiches:

4. Start by spreading garlic herb butter on the bottom slice of white bread and layering on some chips. Spread Spicy Ketchup on the second slice of bread, then sandwich the two slices together.

> **NOTES FOR THE IDIOTS**
>
> Buy the thickest frozen fries you can find if you don't feel like making the chips from scratch. Cook them according to the instructions on the package, then continue on with the sandwich assembly as directed.

EGG SALAD, JAPANESE STYLE

Makes 2 sandwiches
Prep Time: 20 minutes
Cook Time: 15 minutes

INGREDIENTS

Egg Salad:

7 large eggs

½ cup Kewpie mayonnaise

½ teaspoon kosher salt

Pinch of ground white pepper

Pinch of sugar

1 to 2 teaspoons yellow mustard

Sandwich Assembly:

4 slices Japanese milk bread (½ inch thick)

NOTES FOR THE IDIOTS

This is not your grandma's egg salad—set your timer and heed our precise cook time to achieve the coveted "soft yolk." It's perfect.

Kick up the flavor by adding some extra spices and herbs to the egg salad.

The grab-and-go egg salad sandwich, along with its sister, onigiri, are mainstays in the convenience stores (aka konbini) found all over Japan. For good reason—the konbini egg salad sandwich is nothing short of spectacular with its creamy, yolk-laden filling bound together by just enough mayonnaise, and slathered between pillowy slices of milk bread. It's a must-eat on every savvy Japanese tourist's hit list, and a must-make on every savvy idiot chef's cook list. Although we could never perfectly replicate the ones in Japan, ours comes close. Pass the eggs through a sieve to nail the texture and be sure to use Kewpie brand mayonnaise—it's a key ingredient, and easy enough to find these days, so no excuses.

INSTRUCTIONS

Make the Egg Salad:

1. Bring a large saucepan of water to a full boil. Using a slotted spoon, gently place the eggs in the boiling water and set a timer for 7 minutes and 30 seconds.

2. When the timer goes off, remove 2 eggs and plunge them into ice water to stop the cooking process. Leave the remaining eggs in the pot and continue boiling for another 4 minutes.

3. While the remaining eggs cook, take the 2 soft-boiled eggs from the ice water. Peel the eggs and slice each in half lengthwise. The eggs should be cooked with jammy yolks. Set aside with the yolks facing up for assembly.

4. Once the second timer goes off, transfer the remaining eggs to a bowl of cold ice water and let cool for 5 to 10 minutes. Peel the cooled eggs and pass them through a sieve or tamis for a fine mince (optional but adds a luxurious texture—finely chopping your eggs will work too) into a bowl.

5. To the bowl with the minced eggs, add the mayonnaise, salt, white pepper, and sugar. Gradually add mustard to achieve your optimal egg salad taste and consistency.

6. Mix thoroughly and adjust the salt to taste.

Build the Sandwiches:

7. Start by spreading egg salad on two slices of milk bread. Place four soft-boiled egg halves, cut side down, on one slice. Press the two slices together firmly to make a sandwich. Using a serrated knife, carefully trim off the crusts.

SUMMER SQUASH SANDWICH

Makes 4 sandwiches
Prep Time: 30 minutes
Cook Time: 35 minutes

With two squash preparations, a smattering of chopped artichokes, and farm-fresh California goat cheese, this recipe personifies the chic Los Angeles lady. She employs an agent, a manager, and several pool boys. She also loves her power lunches. If you don't have an extra $43 lying around for a grilled vegetable and goat cheese salad at the Ivy but still want to channel your inner diva, make this sandwich immediately.

INGREDIENTS

Artichoke Tapenade:

1½ cups (14.5-ounce jar) artichoke hearts, drained and chopped into large pieces

1 cup (10-ounce jar) green olives, pitted and halved

3 medium garlic cloves, minced

¼ cup capers in brine, drained and chopped

Zest and juice of 1 lemon

1 teaspoon red chile flakes

½ cup extra-virgin olive oil

Melted Yellow Squash:

2 tablespoons neutral oil

2 tablespoons unsalted butter

½ cup thinly sliced small white onion

2 large yellow squash, sliced ⅛ inch thick (about 6 cups)

2 medium garlic cloves, minced

1 tablespoon fresh oregano leaves, minced

1 teaspoon kosher salt

Crispy Zucchini:

1 to 2 cups neutral oil

1 cup all-purpose flour

1 teaspoon kosher salt

½ teaspoon ground black pepper

2 large eggs, whisked

1 cup panko breadcrumbs

¾ cup shredded Parmesan cheese

2 tablespoons minced fresh parsley

6 to 8 zucchini slices, cut lengthwise ¼ inch thick

Sandwich Assembly:

One 10-inch thick Italian loaf, sliced in half lengthwise and warmed

10 ounces goat cheese, softened

1 cup baby kale

continued

INSTRUCTIONS

Make the Artichoke Tapenade:

1. In a medium bowl, combine the artichoke hearts, green olives, garlic, capers, lemon zest and juice, chile flakes, and olive oil. Mix well and reserve for assembly.

Make the Melted Yellow Squash:

2. In a large sauté pan, heat the oil and butter over medium-low heat. Once the butter is melted, add the onions and cook until translucent, 5 to 8 minutes.
3. Add the yellow squash and garlic and cook for another 10 to 15 minutes, until the squash has softened. Finish with the oregano, salt to taste, and reserve for assembly.

Make the Crispy Zucchini:

4. In a countertop fryer or large pot, heat 2 inches of oil over medium-high heat until it reaches 375°F.
5. Set up three shallow dishes: Dish 1: Mix the flour, salt, and pepper. Dish 2: Whisk the eggs. Dish 3: Combine the panko, cheese, and parsley.
6. Dredge the zucchini slices in the seasoned flour, then dip in the egg to coat fully, and finally coat in the cheese-panko mixture, pressing lightly to adhere. Place the breaded zucchini on a plate or sheet tray and repeat the process to coat the remaining zucchini slices.
7. Making sure not to overcrowd the oil, fry a few pieces of breaded zucchini at a time for 2 to 3 minutes on each side, until golden brown and crispy. Remove breaded zucchini and rest over a wire rack to drain excess oil and repeat until all the zucchini is cooked.

Build the Sandwiches:

8. Begin by spreading both halves of the loaf with the goat cheese. Starting on the bottom half, add a layer of crispy zucchini, followed by melted yellow squash, artichoke tapenade, and baby kale. Finish with the Italian loaf top and cut into 4 sandwiches.

THE MORE YOU KNOW
(ABOUT SANDWICHES)

The most expensive sandwich commercially available was the Quintessential Grilled Cheese at Serendipity 3 in New York City. It was made with Dom Pérignon champagne bread, gold flakes, rare cheese made from Italian Podolica cow's milk, white truffles, and a dipping sauce of South African lobster tomato bisque. It is no longer on the menu, but when it was, back in 2014, it cost $214.

NIK BARRICELLI'S SICILIAN STEAK SANDWICH

Makes 4 sandwiches
Prep Time: 20 minutes
Cook Time: 15 minutes

Nik Barricelli is a man of many talents, and lucky for us, one of them is making steak sandwiches. Inspired by a trip to Florence in 2019, he returned home with a single mission—to bring the authentic flavors of Tuscany to the streets of New York. That's why we were so confused when he won our *Idiot Sandwich* competition with this Sicilian steak sandwich, but we aren't ones to resist a perfectly cooked New York strip with crispy baked Parmesan on fresh focaccia. The sirens of Sicily are calling—let's tune in.

INGREDIENTS

Pistachio Tomato Pesto:

¼ cup pistachios, toasted

3 small garlic cloves

⅓ cup shredded Parmesan cheese

1¼ cups fresh basil leaves

1½ tablespoons fresh lemon juice

¼ cup olive oil

1 cup cherry tomatoes

1 teaspoon kosher salt, plus more to taste

Steak:

2 teaspoons neutral oil

Two 12-ounce New York strip or rib eye steaks

2 teaspoons kosher salt

½ teaspoon ground black pepper

4 tablespoons (½ stick) unsalted butter, cold and cubed

4 small sprigs fresh rosemary

Focaccia:

or substitute with any savory herb-dressed focaccia

½ cup olive oil

1 tablespoon chopped fresh parsley leaves

1 tablespoon lemon zest

1 teaspoon red chile flakes

1½ tablespoons honey

1 quarter sheet (9 x 5 inches) plain focaccia, cut in half lengthwise

Sandwich Assembly:

1 cup julienned jarred roasted red peppers

1 cup arugula

2 tablespoons balsamic glaze

Parm Frico (page 209), or substitute with store-bought Parmesan crisps

continued

INSTRUCTIONS

Make the Pistachio Tomato Pesto:

1. In a food processor, combine the toasted pistachios, garlic, and cheese. Process until roughly chopped. Use a rubber spatula as you go to scrape the sides of the bowl to ensure all the ingredients are evenly combined.
2. Add the basil, lemon juice, and 1 tablespoon of the olive oil; pulse to combine. Gradually add the remaining 3 tablespoons of oil while pulsing until the pesto is evenly mixed.
3. Add the cherry tomatoes and pulse until roughly chopped. Add salt to taste and set aside for assembly.

Cook the Steaks:

4. Heat a large cast-iron or sauté pan over high heat and add the oil. Season the steaks with the salt and pepper. Once the oil is shimmering, carefully lay the steaks in the pan. Sear one side for 2 to 3 minutes to develop a nice caramelized crust, then flip and sear the other side for another 2 to 3 minutes. Use tongs to hold the steaks and sear the fat cap and edges for about 2 minutes.
5. Return the steaks to the pan, add the butter and rosemary, and turn the heat to medium. Cook the steaks in the butter, basting for 5 to 8 minutes, until the internal temperature reaches medium rare, 130°F, or to desired doneness. Remove the steaks and let them rest for 5 to 10 minutes before slicing. Wipe out your cast iron and reserve for toasting your focaccia.

Prepare the Focaccia:

6. Heat your cast-iron skillet on medium heat. In a small bowl, mix olive oil, parsley, lemon zest, chile flakes, and honey.
7. Spread the mixture liberally over the top of the focaccia (you can slather it inside as well, if you like) and toast in the pan top side down to seal in the flavor.

Build the Sandwiches:

8. Start with spreading both halves of your focaccia with pistachio tomato pesto. On your bottom half, add steak slices, followed by red bell peppers, Parm Frico, balsamic glaze, and arugula. Finish with the focaccia top and cut into 4 equal sandwiches.

THE MORE YOU KNOW
(ABOUT SANDWICHES)

During World War II, an Italian deli in Connecticut received an order for five hundred hero sandwiches for the US Naval submarine base nearby. From that point forward, they called them subs.

HERBACEOUS CRAB SALAD

Makes 2 sandwiches
Prep Time: 15 minutes
Cook Time: 5 minutes

This Chesapeake Bay–style crab salad has none of the fuss and all the flavor of its more famous counterpart, the Maryland crab cake. Now, we love ourselves a crab cake just as much as the next guy, but there's something about this salad that we love even more—there's no dredging, frying, or big mess to worry about.

INGREDIENTS

Crab Salad:

¼ cup finely diced celery

1 tablespoon minced shallot

2 tablespoons finely diced green bell pepper

¼ cup mayonnaise

2 teaspoons minced fresh parsley

1 tablespoon minced fresh dill

1 tablespoon sliced fresh chives

Zest and juice of ½ lemon

1 teaspoon Dijon mustard

8 ounces cooked jumbo lump crab meat, picked through, removing any shells

Pinch of kosher salt

Pinch of ground black pepper

Sandwich Assembly:

2 brioche lobster roll buns or hot dog buns, lightly toasted with mayonnaise

Picked dill fronds

Zest of 1 lemon

Small handful of butter lettuce leaves, torn as needed to fit the buns

INSTRUCTIONS

Make the Crab Salad:

1. In a medium bowl, combine the celery, shallot, bell pepper, mayonnaise, parsley, dill, chives, lemon zest and juice, and mustard. Mix well.
2. Gently fold in the crab meat, being careful not to break it down too much. Season with the salt and pepper.

Build the Sandwiches:

3. Open the brioche roll and add butter lettuce, crab salad, and dill. Finish with lemon zest.

> **NOTES FOR THE IDIOTS**
> We don't want to tell you what to do, but you *could* make this sandwich with lobster.

ZACH KING'S STEAK BÁNH MÌ

Makes 2 sandwiches
Prep Time: 30 minutes
Cook Time: 20 minutes

INGREDIENTS

Thai Marinated Steak:

6 tablespoons sriracha

6 tablespoons soy sauce

3 tablespoons brown sugar

2 tablespoons fish sauce

1 tablespoon kosher salt

6 tablespoons neutral oil

Two 8-ounce rib eye or New York strip steaks

Spicy Thai Mayo:

½ cup mayonnaise

3 tablespoons sriracha

1 teaspoon fish sauce

1 jalapeño chile, minced

Kosher salt

Sandwich Assembly:

One 10 inch baguette, cut in half lengthwise

Picked cilantro leaves

Thai Pickles (page 212)

Zach King's take on the bánh mì, arguably the most famous of Vietnamese sandwiches, blows our minds almost as much as his magical illusions on social media do. It's the marinated rib eye with the perfectly seared crust that does it. You can't just pull this out of a hat, though (even though Zach made his in twenty minutes on the show). Make quick work of the pickled veggies by using a julienne tool and mix the spicy mayo in advance. Now, go make this sandwich, and then go make it disappear. (By eating it, make it disappear by eating it.)

INSTRUCTIONS

Make the Thai Marinated Steak:

1. In a medium bowl or large zip-top bag, combine the sriracha, soy sauce, brown sugar, fish sauce, salt, and the oil. Add the steak, ensuring it is fully coated with the marinade. Let it marinate for at least 30 minutes.

Make the Spicy Thai Mayo:

2. In a small bowl, combine the mayonnaise, sriracha, fish sauce, and jalapeño. Mix well and season with salt.

Sear the Steak:

3. Preheat a large skillet to medium-high. Remove the steaks from the marinade, pat dry, and place them in the hot skillet. Cook until caramelized and a crust forms, about 2 minutes.

4. Flip the steaks and continue caramelizing for another 2 minutes. Continue to cook and flip until the steaks reach an internal temperature of 125°F. Remove the steaks from the pan and let rest for 10 minutes. Thinly slice the steaks and reserve for assembly.

Build the Sandwiches:

5. Begin by spreading spicy Thai mayo on both halves of the baguette. On the bottom half, layer the steak slices, followed by Thai Pickles and cilantro. Top with the other half of the baguette and cut into two sandwiches.

ONIGIRAZU: A JAPANESE SUSHI SANDWICH

Makes 4 sandwiches
Prep Time: 35 minutes
Cook Time: 35 minutes

INGREDIENTS

Sticky Rice:

2 cups raw sushi rice

2½ cups water

1½ teaspoons kosher salt

5 tablespoons rice vinegar

1½ tablespoons sugar

Pickled Ginger Tuna:

½ cup Kewpie mayonnaise

1 tablespoon minced pickled ginger

1 tablespoon soy sauce

1 scallion, thinly sliced

Pinch of ground black pepper

Pinch of kosher salt, plus more to taste

One 12-ounce can tuna in water, drained and pressed to remove as much of the liquid as possible

Sandwich Assembly:

4 sheets dried nori seaweed sheets

1 avocado, sliced

1 English cucumber, cut in half and julienned

Chili Crisp (page 205), or substitute with store-bought

Finally, a tuna salad we can get behind! Japanese onigirazu is quite similar to onigiri rice ball snacks, except instead of a *ball* of rice, it's more like a *sandwich* of rice, chock full of extra tasty bells and whistles like tuna, cucumber, avocado, and lots of pickled ginger mayo. Sheets of nori act as the "bread," sealing it all together into the cutest little sandwich pocket you've ever laid your eyes on.

INSTRUCTIONS

Make the Sticky Rice (rice cooker method):
or substitute with stovetop rice (instructions below)

1. Rinse the rice under cold water for 1 to 2 minutes, until the water runs clear. Pour the rinsed rice into the rice cooker bowl and add the water and salt. Set the cooker to Cook. In a small saucepan, heat the vinegar and sugar over medium heat, stirring until dissolved. Once the rice is cooked, stir in the vinegar mixture. Spread the cooked rice across a sheet pan and drizzle vinegar mixture over the top. Fold and fluff rice with vinegar mixture to coat evenly. Cool on a sheet pan to room temperature before use.

Make the Sticky Rice (stovetop method):

2. Rinse the rice under cold water for 1 to 2 minutes, until the water runs clear. Combine the rinsed rice, water, and salt in a pot and bring to a boil. Cover the pot and lower the heat to medium-low to maintain a gentle simmer. Cook for 20 minutes without stirring or lifting the lid. Remove the pot from the heat and let it stand, covered, for 10 minutes.

3. In a small saucepan, heat the vinegar and sugar over medium heat, stirring until dissolved. After resting, spread the rice across a sheet pan and season with the vinegar. Fold and fluff rice with vinegar mixture to coat evenly. Cool on sheet pan to room temperature before use.

continued

Make the Pickled Ginger Tuna:

4. In a small bowl, begin by making the pickled ginger mayonnaise. Mix the mayonnaise, pickled ginger, soy sauce, scallions, pepper, and salt.
5. Put the drained and pressed tuna in another bowl and incrementally mix in the pickled ginger mayo until you reach your desired consistency. Adjust the salt to taste.

Build the Sandwich:

6. Lay a sheet of plastic wrap on a flat surface, about double the size of your nori sheet. Place the nori sheet on top, shiny side down.
7. Wet your fingers with cold water to prevent the rice from sticking.
8. In the center of the nori, spread about ¼ cup of sushi rice into a diamond shape.
9. Top with just under ¼ cup of the tuna mixture, one-quarter of the avocado slices, and an equal amount of cucumber slices.
10. Cover with another layer of sushi rice, adjusting the amount as needed.
11. Carefully bring the two opposite corners of the nori to the center, then bring the other two corners together to form a square.
12. Wrap tightly with plastic wrap and let it rest for 5 to 10 minutes in the refrigerator to allow the nori to adhere.
13. Cut in half and serve with Chili Crisp.

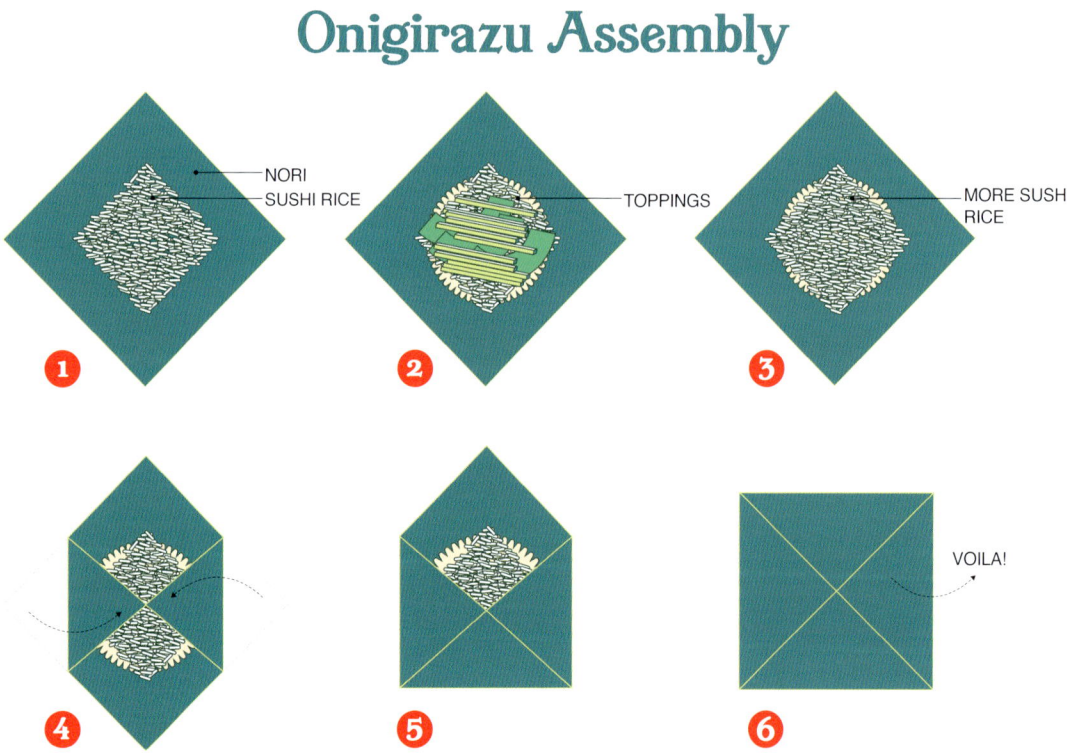

FALAFEL PITA

Makes 4 pita sandwiches
Prep Time: 45 minutes
Cook Time: 10 minutes

Pitas have been around since the Stone Age, since the invention of the wheel, in fact. Now that we think of it, pitas are wheel-shaped. Hmmm, spooky. Anyway, it would be thousands of years before falafel and hummus would enter the picture, but that is still hundreds of years ago. Our take is anything that's been around for this long must be good, and there's no need to reinvent the wheel, or the pita, for this one. So, we didn't. Please enjoy this classic, ancient sando.

INGREDIENTS

Falafel:

Two 15-ounce cans chickpeas, drained

¼ cup chopped onion

¾ cup chopped fresh parsley leaves

¾ cup chopped fresh cilantro leaves

3 medium garlic cloves, chopped

⅔ cup all-purpose flour

¾ teaspoon kosher salt

2 teaspoons ground cumin

¼ teaspoon ground black pepper

¼ teaspoon cayenne pepper

½ teaspoon baking powder

1 to 2 quarts neutral oil, for frying

Hummus:

One 15-ounce can chickpeas, drained (reserve liquid for later use)

¼ cup tahini

Zest and juice of 2 lemons

3 small garlic cloves

3 tablespoons extra-virgin olive oil

¾ teaspoon kosher salt, plus more to taste

Cucumber Parsley Salad:

¼ cup extra-virgin olive oil

¼ cup fresh lemon juice

½ teaspoon kosher salt

1½ cups chopped fresh parsley (1 to 2 bunches)

½ cup sliced (half-moon) Persian or English cucumber

½ cup seeded and finely diced tomato

¼ cup chopped fresh mint

1 scallion, thinly sliced

Sandwich Assembly:

2 pitas, halved and warmed

12 to 16 falafels

Garlic Sauce (page 195)

continued

INSTRUCTIONS

Prepare the Falafel Dough:

1. In a food processor, pulse the drained chickpeas, onion, parsley, cilantro, garlic, flour, salt, cumin, black pepper, cayenne, and baking powder until well combined. Scrape the sides as needed to incorporate evenly. Transfer the mixture to a bowl, cover with plastic wrap, and refrigerate for at least 1 hour and up to overnight.
2. Form the falafels into balls using about 2 tablespoons of mixture. The mixture will make about 12 to 16 falafels. Place on a lined sheet tray until ready to fry. The falafel dough balls can be frozen for future use for up to 1 month.

Make the Hummus:

3. In a food processor, combine the chickpeas, tahini, lemon zest, lemon juice, and garlic and process to a paste. Slowly add olive oil through the top of the processor; the hummus should be thick like a paste but still spreadable. If it's too thick, adjust with some of the reserved canned chickpea liquid. Season with salt to taste.

Make the Cucumber Parsley Salad:

4. In a large bowl, whisk the olive oil, lemon juice, and salt. Add the parsley, cucumber, tomato, mint, and scallion. Toss to combine, and adjust the salt to taste.

Fry the Falafel:

5. In a countertop fryer or large pot, heat at least 3 inches of neutral oil over medium-high heat to 375°F. Add the falafel, in batches so as not to overcrowd the pot, and fry for about 5 minutes, until golden brown on the outside. Drain on paper towels. Serve hot.

Build the Sandwiches:

6. Fill the pita pocket with hummus, ¼ cup of cucumber parsley salad, and three to four falafels. Serve with Garlic Sauce.

NOTES FOR THE IDIOTS

Substitute premade frozen falafels from the grocery store, or a packaged falafel mix. Follow the package's mixing instructions before frying in step 5. You can also use store-bought hummus and garlic sauce instead of homemade, if you need a quick shortcut.

FISH, NO CHIPS

Makes 4 sandwiches
Prep Time: 15 minutes
Cook Time: 20 minutes

INGREDIENTS

Beer-Battered Fish:

Neutral oil, for frying

3 cups all-purpose flour

¾ cup cornstarch

1½ teaspoons baking soda

1 tablespoon kosher salt, plus more to season fish

One 12-ounce bottle pilsner or other favorite beer

2 cups all-purpose flour, for dredging

1½ pounds cod fillets, cut into four 6-ounce portions, or substitute with any firm white fish, such as rockfish, halibut, or haddock

Sandwich Assembly:

4 potato buns, cut in half lengthwise and toasted

½ cup Avocado Green Goddess (page 194), or substitute with store-bought

6 leaves baby gem or butter leaf lettuce

Here is our ode to fish and chips, the most British dish that ever was. We removed the chips because this sandwich is already so crispy, crunchy, flaky, and delicious that it really doesn't need them—we like to work smarter, not harder—plus, we already put chips in a different sandwich (the Chip Butty, page 79, which you simply must try). For the full fish and chips experience, we recommend you make both sandwiches and shove them into your mouth at the same time.

INSTRUCTIONS

Fry the Beer-Battered Fish:

1. Preheat a countertop fryer or large pot with oil. You want to have enough oil to completely submerge your fish pieces.
2. Combine 1 cup of the flour, the cornstarch, baking soda, and salt in a medium bowl. Whisk in the beer until smooth. It should resemble pancake batter.
3. Pat the fish fillets dry and season lightly with salt. Put the remaining 2 cups flour on a separate plate and dredge each fillet in the flour, shaking off excess, then dip in the beer batter, making sure the fish is fully covered in batter.
4. Carefully dip half of the fish into the hot oil, moving it back and forth 4 or 5 times before fully dropping it in to avoid it sticking to the bottom of the pot.
5. Fry for about 5 minutes, until golden brown on the outside and the internal temperature reaches 140°F.
6. Remove the crispy battered fish from the oil and drain on a rack to keep it crispy. Season with salt before serving.

Build the Sandwiches:

7. Start by spreading Avocado Green Goddess dressing on both halves of the bun. On the bottom half, layer baby gem lettuce, then add the beer-battered fish. Top with the other half of the bun.

MATT STONIE'S MISSISSIPPI SHRIMP SLUGBURGER

Makes 4 sandwiches
Prep Time: 40 minutes
Cook Time: 15 minutes

INGREDIENTS

Shrimp Patties:

1 pound shrimp, peeled and deveined

¼ cup cornmeal, plus about ¼ cup more to coat the shrimp cakes

2 teaspoons kosher salt

½ teaspoon ground black pepper

3 tablespoons minced fresh chives

2 tablespoons minced red onion

¼ cup neutral oil

Sandwich Assembly:

4 brioche buns, cut in half lengthwise and toasted

Yellow mustard

Pickled Red Onion (page 213), or substitute with store-bought pickled red onions

Dill pickle chips

Spicy Cajun Mayo (page 201), optional

There are only two things you need to know about Matt Stonie:

1. He won the Nathan's Hot Dog Eating Competition in 2015 by downing 62 hot dogs in 10 minutes.
2. He won the official *Idiot Sandwich* Shrimp Competition in 2024 with this recipe—his take on a Mississippi Slugburger.

His uses shrimp instead of the typical beef or pork, and he adds some pickled red onions for zing. He only made one on the show, but we're pretty sure he can eat them by the dozen, which is how many you'll want to eat after your first bite.

INSTRUCTIONS

Cook the Shrimp Patties:

1. Finely mince half of the shrimp on a cutting board until almost paste-like. Slice the remaining shrimp into ¼-inch pieces to give added texture to your shrimp patties.
2. In a large bowl, combine the minced shrimp, sliced shrimp, ¼ cup of the cornmeal, the salt, pepper, chives, and onion and mix evenly. Divide the mixture into 4 equal portions and shape it into patties about ½ inch thick and the diameter of your buns. Dust the patties in the remaining ¼ cup cornmeal on all sides.
3. Heat a large skillet over medium heat and add the oil. Once the oil is shimmering, carefully add the shrimp patties. Cook for about 3 minutes, until golden brown, then flip and cook for another 3 minutes, or until crisp and golden on both sides and the internal temperature reaches 145°F. Remove the patties from the pan and set on rack.

Build the Sandwiches:

4. Spread yellow mustard on both halves of the brioche bun. On the bottom half, layer a shrimp patty, dill pickles, and Pickled Red Onions, then top with the other half of the bun.

PASTRAMI SALMON

Makes 2 sandwiches
Prep Time: 15 minutes
Cook Time: 10 minutes

INGREDIENTS

Dill and Lemon Cream Cheese:

¼ cup cream cheese, softened

Zest and juice of 1 lemon

1 tablespoon chopped fresh dill

Pinch of kosher salt

Pinch of ground black pepper

Pastrami Salmon:

1 tablespoon dark brown sugar

1 teaspoon kosher salt

1 teaspoon garlic powder

1 teaspoon ground ginger

1 teaspoon ground coriander

1 teaspoon ground black pepper

½ teaspoon ground allspice

12-ounce salmon fillet, skin and pin bones removed

2 tablespoons olive oil

1 lemon

Sandwich Assembly:

4 slices rye bread, lightly toasted

Picked dill fronds

¼ cup Pickled Red Onion (page 213), or substitute with store-bought

Not all pastrami must be made from beef. Repeat after us: If you can dream it, then you can pastrami it. All you have to do is coat your dream in the typical pastrami spice blend, and from there, the world is your oyster. Mmmmmm pastrami oysters . . . For this, we pastrami the hell out of some salmon, then, instead of smoking it like beef, we blacken it, slather it in dill cream cheese, and serve it up on some rye, like a proper dream weaver should.

INSTRUCTIONS

Make the Dill and Lemon Cream Cheese:

1. In a small bowl, mix together cream cheese, lemon zest and juice, and dill. Season with the salt and pepper and set aside for assembly.

Cook the Pastrami Salmon:

2. In a small bowl, combine the brown sugar, salt, garlic powder, ginger, coriander, pepper, and allspice. Season the salmon on all sides with the spice mixture, pressing the spices into the salmon, and let rest for 10 to 20 minutes to allow the flavors to penetrate. Slice the salmon lengthwise into ½-inch-thick uniform strips, ensuring the seasoning remains on the outer surface of each piece.

3. Heat the olive oil in a large skillet over medium heat. Once shimmering, place the salmon slices, pink sides down, in a row across the pan. Zest one-quarter of the lemon over the salmon and cook until it is caramelized on one side, about 2 minutes. Flip the salmon and zest another quarter of the lemon over it.

4. Once the salmon is caramelized, remove from the heat and squeeze the lemon over it. Remove from the pan and let the salmon rest on a paper towel–lined plate for a couple minutes before assembly.

Build the Sandwiches:

5. Spread dill and lemon cream cheese on two slices of rye. On one slice, layer on salmon slices, followed by Pickled Red Onions and dill fronds and top with your second slice.

NIGHT

We know what real idiots want, and we made these sandwiches just for you. Whether it's a croque monsieur sizzling in a creamy béchamel sauce, or a meatball sandwich that practically melts in your mouth, these sandwiches are so hot, so doused in unctuous goodness, that there's only one time you should eat them, and that's after dark. C'mon, let us show you our most intimate recipe fantasies, so you can eat these sandwiches all . . . night . . . long.

Ahem. Okay. All apologies, we got a little carried away. It's just that these sandwiches are really doing it for us, and we know they'll do it for you, too. You see, it takes a little time to do night sandwiches right. It's best if you go slow, but it's worth the wait. The rush of the day is over. You finally get to snuggle up on the couch in the softest of pants, flip on the TV or your favorite podcast, and go to town on a Spicy Korean Chicken Sando (page 106), which just so happens to be one of Gordon's favorites. Or maybe it's the hot, juicy Italian Beef (page 147) you want. No matter, you aren't here to impress anyone, and we aren't here to judge. Let those fillings fall all over; take a beat before you wipe your chin. Relax. We won't tell anyone if you eat with your hands. Tender is the night and tender are these sammies. It's time to reap the rewards of a day well lived. It's time for *Night Sandwiches*.

Spicy Korean Chicken Sando   106

Short Rib Toastie   108

Greek Turkey Meatball   110

Braised Lamb and Feta   113

Blackened Salmon   117

Kofta Pita   118

Achiote Pork   120

Cauliflower Katsu   123

Broccoli Cheddar Melt   125

Albert Niazhvinski's Wellington Sando   126

Tonkatsu Cubano   129

Currywurst   131

Pulled Pork Sliders   132

Grilled Eggplant Caponata   135

Pineapple Jerk Chicken   138

Brisket Sandwich   141

Chicken French Dip   145

Italian Beef   147

Croque Monsieur   151

Steak and Chimichurri   153

Peri-Peri Chicken   155

Josh Scherer's Carne Asada Cheesesteak   157

SPICY KOREAN CHICKEN SANDO

Makes 2 sandwiches
Prep Time: 2½ hours (including marinating time)
Cook Time: 20 minutes

We don't like to toot our own horn, but we are always happy to toot Gordon's. He made this sandwich when he hit forty million followers on TikTok. From the gochujang honey glaze on the fried chicken, all the way down to the kimchi mayo and coleslaw, this is clearly his preferred celebration sando, and now it can be yours, too.

INGREDIENTS

Chicken Marinade:
2 cups buttermilk

2 teaspoons garlic powder

2 teaspoons Korean chile flakes

1 teaspoon kosher salt

Two 6- to 8-ounce boneless, skinless chicken thighs

Gochujang Honey Glaze:
¼ cup honey

2 tablespoons gochujang paste, plus more to taste

Chicken Dredge:
2 quarts neutral oil, for frying

1 cup all-purpose flour

¾ cup potato starch or cornstarch

2 teaspoons garlic powder

2 teaspoons Korean chile flakes or other red chile flakes

2 teaspoons kosher salt

½ teaspoon ground black pepper

Kimchi Mayo:
½ cup finely chopped kimchi

½ cup Japanese mayonnaise, such as Kewpie

1 tablespoon soy sauce

Slaw:
2 cups grated red cabbage (grated on a box grater)

Juice of 1 lemon

Sandwich Assembly:
2 potato buns, sliced in half lengthwise and toasted

3 tablespoons unsalted butter, softened

Dill pickle slices

INSTRUCTIONS

Marinate the Chicken:
1. In a large bowl, whisk together the buttermilk, garlic powder, chile flakes, and salt. Add the chicken thighs and toss to coat completely. Marinate in a zip-top bag or covered bowl and refrigerate for at least 2 hours or up to overnight.

Make the Gochujang Honey Glaze:
1. In a small saucepan, combine the honey and gochujang and place over medium heat. Bring to a simmer, then remove from the heat and set aside.

Make the Kimchi Mayo:

1. In a small bowl, whisk the kimchi, mayonnaise, and soy sauce to combine. Set aside and reserve for assembly.

Fry the Chicken:

2. In a countertop fryer or large pot over medium heat, bring the neutral oil to 350°F. In a shallow dish, mix together the flour, cornstarch, garlic powder, chile flakes, salt, and pepper.
3. Remove the chicken from the marinade and let the excess liquid drip off. Place the chicken in the flour mixture and toss to coat completely. Shake off excess flour and carefully place the chicken into the hot oil, making sure not to overcrowd. Fry the chicken until the crust turns golden brown and it reaches an internal temperature of 165°F, about 8 minutes.
4. Carefully remove the chicken from the oil and place on a wire rack to rest for 5 minutes. When ready to assemble, toss the chicken in the Gochujang Honey Glaze to coat completely.

Make the Slaw:

5. In a medium bowl, combine the shredded cabbage and lemon juice. Massage the cabbage until it is tender.

Build the Sandwiches:

6. Spread kimchi mayo on both halves of the potato bun. On the bottom half, layer slaw, gochujang honey–glazed fried chicken, and pickles, then top with the other half of the bun.

SHORT RIB TOASTIE

Makes 2 sandwiches

Prep Time: 15 minutes

Cook Time: 4 hours

INGREDIENTS

Braised Short Ribs:

2 tablespoons neutral oil

3 thick-cut beef short ribs (1¼ pounds bone-in short ribs)

1 tablespoon kosher salt

2 teaspoons ground black pepper

2 tablespoons all-purpose flour

3 large garlic cloves, smashed

½ large yellow onion, chopped

1 celery stalk, chopped

1 large carrot, chopped

4 sprigs thyme

1 tablespoon tomato paste

1 cup red wine

1 quart beef broth

Sandwich Assembly:

4 slices thick-cut sourdough bread

3 tablespoons mayonnaise

4 slices Gruyère cheese

Spicy Tomato and Mushroom Chutney (page 198)

4 slices cheddar cheese

We've been giving the Brits a hard time throughout this entire book, but that ends here, with the arrival of the toastie—a type of sandwich so delicious, even the English can't mess it up. Toasties are basically the same as an American grilled cheese, except they are almost always pressed, and they usually have other ingredients beyond cheese, just like this recipe right here, with its slow-braised short ribs and tomato mushroom chutney. And to any British folks who might be reading this, the answer is no, you should *not* substitute jellied eels for the short ribs in this recipe.

INSTRUCTIONS

Braise the Short Ribs:

1. Preheat the oven to 325°F. Heat a Dutch oven or roasting pan over high heat and add the oil. Season the short ribs with the salt and pepper. Toss with the flour. Once the oil is shimmering, sear the beef for 3 to 5 minutes on each side, until browned, then remove from the pan and set aside.

2. Add the garlic, onion, celery, carrot, and thyme to the pan and cook over high heat until golden and aromatic, about 5 minutes. Stir in the tomato paste and cook for another 2 minutes to caramelize the tomato paste. Deglaze the pan with the wine, scraping the bits from the bottom. Bring to a boil and cook for about 10 minutes, until the wine is reduced by half.

3. Return the seared short ribs to the pan and then add the broth, ensuring the meat is covered by the braising liquid.

4. Cover the pan and braise in the oven for 3½ to 4 hours, until the meat is tender. Remove meat from the oven and allow to cool slightly. Once cool enough to be handled, shred the meat and return it to the braising liquid until ready for assembly.

NOTES FOR THE IDIOTS

Using store-bought braised beef will cut the cook time by 3½ hours or more.

Cook the Sandwiches:

5. Preheat a medium skillet on medium heat. Lightly spread each slice of bread with mayonnaise. With the mayo on the bottom begin layering 2 slices of gruyere, Spicy Tomato and Mushroom Chutney, warm short rib meat, and top with two slices of cheddar cheese.
6. Place the second piece of bread on top with the mayonnaise spread on the outside and press down on the sandwich to adhere the two halves. Gently lay sandwich in pan and toast each side to golden brown, about 90 second per side.

THE MORE YOU KNOW
(ABOUT SANDWICHES)

School cafeterias began pairing tomato soup with grilled cheese after World War II to hit the target vitamin C requirements, and it stuck.

GREEK TURKEY MEATBALL

Makes 4 sandwiches
Prep Time: 20 minutes
Cook Time: 35 minutes

You can't make a cookbook about sandwiches and not include a meatball hoagie. That would be irresponsible and, dare we say . . . idiotic. But we like to buck convention. Some might say that everything the Italians did, the Greeks did better, citing examples of mythology, olive oil, and sometimes even little balls of meat. So, here's our Greek version of the Italian meatball sandwich. Now with 10 percent more tzatziki!

INGREDIENTS

Tzatziki:
or substitute with store-bought tzatziki
¾ cup whole milk Greek yogurt
¼ cup finely grated cucumber, salted and drained
¼ teaspoon finely minced garlic
1 teaspoon lemon zest
1 tablespoon fresh lemon juice
2 tablespoons chopped fresh dill

Turkey Meatballs:
1 pound ground turkey meat
¼ cup finely diced white onion
¼ cup Italian breadcrumbs
¼ cup whole milk
1 large egg
2 tablespoons chopped fresh mint
2 tablespoons dried oregano
Zest of 1 lemon
2 teaspoons kosher salt
¼ teaspoon ground black pepper
2 tablespoons neutral oil

Greek Tomato Sauce:
1 tablespoon olive oil
⅓ cup finely chopped red onion
4 medium garlic cloves, chopped
1 teaspoon red chile flakes
24 ounces tomato passata
1 tablespoon chopped fresh dill
2 tablespoons chopped fresh parsley leaves
¼ cup kalamata olives, pitted and halved

Sandwich Assembly:
4 crusty hoagie rolls, hinged and toasted
4 to 6 tablespoons feta crumbles
3 cups baby spinach
Kosher salt
Ground black pepper

continued

INSTRUCTIONS

Make the Tzatziki:

1. In a small bowl, add the grated cucumber and sprinkle lightly with salt. Let cucumbers sit for 20 to 30 minutes while the moisture seeps. Squeeze cucumbers of any excess water.
2. Mix together the yogurt, grated cucumber, garlic, lemon zest and juice, and dill in a small bowl until thoroughly combined. Season to taste with salt and pepper. Let the tzatziki marinate in the refrigerator for 30 minutes before serving.

Make the Turkey Meatballs:

3. In a medium bowl, combine the ground turkey, onions, breadcrumbs, milk, egg, mint, oregano, lemon zest, salt, and pepper. Mix until fully combined. Wet your hands to prevent sticking and roll the mixture into 16 meatballs, each roughly just under the size of a golf ball, and place them on a sheet tray.
4. Preheat a large skillet over medium-high heat and add the oil to the pan. When oil shimmers, add the meatballs in a single layer. Move the meatballs as they cook so the outsides are evenly browned and caramelized, about 10 minutes. Remove from the pan and set aside while you build your sauce.

Make the Greek Tomato Sauce:

5. In a small saucepan, heat the olive oil over medium-high heat. Add the onion and sauté for about 5 minutes, until slightly caramelized and translucent. Add the garlic and chile flakes and continue to sauté for another 2 to 3 minutes, until the garlic is fragrant. Stir in the tomato passata, bring to a simmer, and cook for another 10 to 15 minutes.
6. Add the dill, parsley, and olives and stir them into the sauce. Add the salt and pepper and adjust seasoning to taste. Gently add the meatballs to the sauce, spooning some sauce over the top. Cook for an additional 10 minutes, or until the meatballs are fully cooked through and reach an internal temperature of 165°F. Keep warm until assembly.

Build the Sandwiches:

7. Open your hoagie roll and spread tzatziki on the top half. On the bottom half, add a couple of spoonfuls of tomato sauce, followed by baby spinach, four turkey meatballs, and more tomato sauce. Sprinkle with feta crumbles, then close the roll and enjoy.

BRAISED LAMB AND FETA

Makes 4 sandwiches
Prep Time: 20 to 25 minutes
Cook Time: 3 hours

This recipe is all about the chermoula, which is an herbaceous North African green sauce similar to chimichurri (more on that on page 195). We use lamb here, but if you don't like it, or if you are strapped for time, pick up any type of braised meat from the store. Short ribs or a chuck roast would be great. Heck, you could even make this with chicken. Just don't sleep on that chermoula, please.

INGREDIENTS

Braised Lamb Shanks:

3 pounds lamb shanks, or substitute with any braised beef or chicken

½ cup all-purpose flour

¼ cup neutral oil

1 yellow onion, quartered

1 carrot, cut into large chunks

5 medium garlic cloves, smashed

12 sprigs fresh thyme

2 teaspoons tomato paste

4 teaspoons harissa paste

1 whole lemon, cut into 4 pieces

1½ quarts beef broth

Sumac Onions:

½ red onion, thinly sliced

1 tablespoon minced fresh parsley

2 pinches of sumac

1 tablespoon extra-virgin olive oil

2 teaspoons fresh lemon juice

Chermoula:

1 cup fresh parsley leaves and tender stems

1 cup fresh cilantro leaves and tender stems

2 medium garlic cloves

1 teaspoon ground coriander

1 teaspoon red chile flakes

½ teaspoon paprika

½ teaspoon ground ginger

¼ teaspoon saffron threads, optional

Zest and juice of 1 lemon

¾ cup extra-virgin olive oil

Sandwich Assembly:

4 slices sourdough bread, toasted

½ cup baby arugula

Whipped Feta (page 198)

Kosher salt

Ground black pepper

continued

INSTRUCTIONS

Braise the Lamb Shanks:

1. Preheat the oven to 350°F. Season the lamb shanks generously with the salt and pepper and coat them in the flour. Heat the neutral oil in a 6- to 8-quart Dutch oven or large pot with a lid over high heat. Sear the lamb shanks until browned on all sides, then remove them from the pot and set aside.

2. Add the onion, carrot, garlic, and thyme to the same pot. Cook over high heat until golden and aromatic. Stir in the tomato paste and cook for about 2 minutes to caramelize the paste, then add the harissa and lemon. Add the stock and return the lamb shanks to the pot and bring to a simmer. Cover with a lid and braise in the oven for 2 to 3 hours, until the lamb is tender.

3. Once lamb is cooked and tender, let the lamb cool to room temperature in the braising liquid. Skim off excess fat and remove the cooked shanks from the pot. Use a sieve to strain and discard large chunks of vegetables and herbs (it doesn't have to be perfectly strained). Over medium-high heat, reduce the braising liquid by at least half, or until it coats the back of a spoon, about 15 minutes. Turn the heat down to low, gently shred the lamb into large chunks, and add it to the reduced lamb jus to warm for assembly. Season meat to taste.

Make the Sumac Onions:

4. In a small bowl, combine the sliced onions with the parsley, sumac, 2 pinches of salt, olive oil, and lemon juice. Toss to coat and let marinate 10 to 15 minutes or until ready to use.

Make the Chermoula:

5. In a food processor, combine the parsley, cilantro, garlic, coriander, chile flakes, paprika, ginger, saffron threads, and a pinch of salt. Add the lemon zest and juice and pulse to combine. While pulsing, drizzle the olive oil through the top opening until a coarse, chunky consistency is achieved. Season with additional salt to taste.

Build the Sandwiches:

6. Spread Whipped Feta on both halves of the sourdough. On the bottom half, layer braised lamb, drizzle with chermoula, and add baby arugula and sumac onions. Top with the other half of the sourdough to complete the sandwich.

BLACKENED SALMON

Makes 4 sandwiches
Prep Time: 10 minutes
Cook Time: 30 minutes

Sometimes all you need is a little ranch dressing to get through the day. In this sandwich, the ranch mellows the heat from the blackening spices and creates the perfect lake of sauce for the salmon to swim in. Of course, we recommend making it from scratch, but you can totally substitute with store-bought dressing in a pinch.

INGREDIENTS

Roasted Red Onion:
8 slices red onion rings (¼ inch thick)

1 tablespoon neutral oil

Blackened Salmon:
Four 8-ounce pieces salmon, skin and pin bones removed

1 tablespoon neutral oil

2 tablespoons blackening spice

3 tablespoons cold unsalted butter

Arugula:
1½ cups baby arugula

Juice of ½ lemon

1 teaspoon olive oil

Sandwich Assembly:
4 brioche buns, sliced in half lengthwise, toasted

Buttermilk Ranch (page 194), or substitute with store-bought ranch dressing

Kosher salt

Ground black pepper

INSTRUCTIONS

Roast the Red Onion:
1. Preheat the oven to 375°F. Place the onion rings on a sheet tray. Drizzle with the oil and season with salt and pepper. Roast in the oven for about 15 minutes, until tender and slightly charred. Remove from the oven and reserve for assembly.

Sear the Salmon:
2. Preheat a large nonstick pan over medium heat and add the oil. Season the salmon with the blackening spice. Once the oil is shimmering, sear for 3 to 5 minutes on each side, until the salmon is caramelized, but be sure not to let it burn.

3. Add the butter and baste the salmon for 3 to 5 minutes, until it reaches an internal temperature of 120°F. The total time for your salmon will depend on the thickness, so adjust accordingly. Remove the salmon from the pan and let it rest until assembly.

Toss the Arugula:
4. In a small bowl, toss the arugula with the lemon juice and olive oil. Season with salt and pepper.

Build the Sandwiches:
5. Spread Buttermilk Ranch on both halves of the brioche bun. On the bottom half, add blackened salmon, roasted red onions, and arugula, then top with the other half of the bun.

KOFTA PITA

Makes 4 sandwiches
Prep Time: 40 minutes
Cook Time: 20 minutes

Kofta is a Middle Eastern dish of ground meat, often lamb, that's mixed with tons of fragrant spices. From there it can be formed any number of ways before it's grilled to perfection. We suggest molding yours onto a skewer for ultimate kebab vibes, but truth be told, we've never met a kofta we didn't like, and we're certain you'll fall in love with this one no matter what shape it takes. Especially after you stuff it in a pita and smother it with some spicy red zhoug and garlic sauce.

INGREDIENTS

Sumac Onions:

½ cup thinly sliced red onion

2 pinches of sumac

1 tablespoon extra-virgin olive oil

1 tablespoon finely chopped fresh parsley

Red Zhoug Sauce:

1½ cups chopped red bell pepper

2 red jalapeño chiles, seeds removed, chopped

1 tablespoon paprika

2 tablespoons chopped fresh cilantro

1 tablespoon fresh lemon juice

2 teaspoons ground cumin

3 small garlic cloves

¼ cup olive oil

Kofta:

1 pound ground lamb

1 pound ground beef

⅓ cup finely diced onion

3 medium garlic cloves, minced

½ cup fresh parsley leaves, minced

1½ teaspoons ground allspice

1½ teaspoons ground cumin

½ teaspoon ground cinnamon

½ teaspoon ground cardamom

1 teaspoon paprika

2 tablespoons kosher salt

1 tablespoon neutral oil

Sandwich Assembly:

2 pitas, cut in half, opening each half in the center to form a pocket

16 to 20 thin slices Persian or English cucumber

4 romaine lettuce leaves

Garlic Sauce (page 195), or substitute with store-bought garlic sauce

Kosher salt

INSTRUCTIONS

Make the Sumac Onions:

1. In a small bowl, mix together the onion, sumac, olive oil, 2 pinches of salt, and parsley and let marinate while you work on the other components.

Make the Red Zhoug Sauce:

2. In a food processor, combine the bell pepper, chiles, paprika, cilantro, lemon juice, cumin, garlic, and a pinch of salt and process to combine. Drizzle in the oil through the top of the processor until the mixture has a slightly chunky consistency (it shouldn't become a paste). Scrape down the sides of the bowl with a rubber spatula for an even blend. Adjust seasoning to taste.

Prep and Grill the Kofta:

3. In a medium bowl, thoroughly mix the ground lamb, ground beef, onion, garlic, parsley, allspice, cumin, cinnamon, cardamom, paprika, and salt.

4. Portion the mixture into 1½- to 2-ounce, 3-inch logs. Thread onto 6-inch metal skewers or soaked bamboo skewers.

5. Preheat a grill pan over medium-high heat and coat with the neutral oil. Grill the skewers on all sides for about 8 minutes total, until caramelized and the internal temperature reaches 160°F. Remove the koftas from the skewers and set aside for sandwich assembly.

Build the Sandwiches:

6. Fill the pita pocket with red zhoug sauce, romaine lettuce, and three to four koftas. Add in four to five slices of cucumber, followed by sumac onions and the Garlic Sauce.

ACHIOTE PORK

Makes 4 sandwiches
Prep Time: 4 hours
(includes marinating of pork)
Cook Time: 25 minutes

Achiote is a common ingredient in Mexican and Caribbean food. Made from annatto seeds that are ground into a brick-colored paste, the flavor is quite mild, but what it lacks in pungency, it more than makes up for in color, as it stains everything it touches red—including your skin. It's inexpensive and easy to find in most grocery stores, plus it's the whole point of this sandwich, so don't skip it. This is probably the only time we will ever encourage you to get caught red-handed.

INGREDIENTS

Achiote Marinated Pork:

½ cup orange juice concentrate (found in the frozen food aisle)

1½ tablespoons fresh lime juice

3 tablespoons achiote paste

1 tablespoon ground cumin

1 tablespoon kosher salt

1 tablespoon ground coriander

1 teaspoon ground black pepper

1 tablespoon Mexican oregano

6 garlic cloves, minced

1½ tablespoons honey

1½ to 2 pounds pork tenderloin, trimmed of silver skin

2 tablespoons neutral oil

Avocado Smash:

2 ripe avocados

¼ cup Salsa Verde (page 196), or substitute with store-bought salsa verde

2 teaspoons chopped fresh cilantro

Kosher salt

Ground black pepper

Sandwich Assembly:

4 bolillo rolls, sliced in half lengthwise

2 cups shredded iceberg lettuce

Pickled Red Onion (page 213), or substitute with store-bought

Salsa Verde (page 196), or substitute with store-bought

INSTRUCTIONS

Marinate and Sear the Achiote Pork:

1. In a blender, combine the orange juice concentrate, lime juice, achiote paste, cumin, salt, coriander, pepper, oregano, garlic, and honey. Blend until smooth.

2. Place the pork tenderloin in a resealable plastic bag or bowl and pour the marinade over it. Remove as much air as possible before sealing the bag. Marinate in the refrigerator for at least 4 hours or overnight.

3. Preheat the oven to 425°F. Heat a large sauté pan over medium-high heat and add the neutral oil. Remove the pork from the marinade, letting the excess drip off, and reserve the remaining marinade. Sear the pork in the pan for 3 to 4 minutes, until browned, then flip and sear for another 3 to 4 minutes.

4. Transfer the pork to a roasting pan and pour the reserved marinade over it. Cook for about 20 to 25 minutes or until the internal temperature reaches 140°F. Remove from the oven and let the pork rest for 15 minutes. Cut the pork into 1/8-inch slices. Return the sliced pork to the roasting pan juices and reserve for assembly.

Make the Avocado Smash:

5. In a small bowl, lightly mash the avocado with the Salsa Verde. Stir in the cilantro and season with salt and pepper.

Build the Sandwiches:

6. Spread avocado smash on the bottom half of the bolillo roll. Layer on achiote pork, drizzle with Salsa Verde, add Pickled Red Onions, and finish with iceberg lettuce. Top with the other half of the roll.

CAULIFLOWER KATSU

Makes 4 sandwiches
Prep Time: 20 minutes
Cook Time: 15 minutes

We strongly believe that a cauliflower steak can be just as good, if not better, than its meaty counterpart, and we also know that a katsu sando needn't be comprised of animals. So, we decided to combine those two beliefs and make a vegetarian meal that all the meat-eaters will love. May your cauliflower katsu be the crispiest in town, and may they forever remain as tasty as the pork ones.

INGREDIENTS

Tonkatsu Sauce:

½ cup tonkatsu sauce (found in the Asian foods aisle)

1 tablespoon sriracha

½ teaspoon fresh lemon juice

Cauliflower Katsu:

1 to 2 cups neutral oil, for frying

1 cup all-purpose flour

1 tablespoon garlic salt

1 teaspoon ground black pepper

3 large eggs, beaten

3 cups panko breadcrumbs

2 medium heads cauliflower, cut into ½-inch steaks (4 steaks are needed)

Kosher salt

Cabbage:

1 cup thinly sliced green cabbage

1 tablespoon kosher salt

¼ cup Kewpie mayonnaise

Sandwich Assembly:

8 slices milk bread (½ inch thick), lightly toasted on one side

INSTRUCTIONS

Make the Tonkatsu Sauce:

1. In a small bowl, whisk together tonkatsu sauce, sriracha, and lemon juice. Reserve for assembly.

Make the Cauliflower Katsu:

2. Heat 2 inches of oil in a large skillet over medium heat to 350°F. Prepare three shallow dishes: Dish 1: Combine the flour, garlic salt, and pepper; mix thoroughly. Dish 2: Whisk the eggs. Dish 3: Dump in the panko.

3. Coat the cauliflower steaks in the seasoned flour, tossing to cover completely. Remove and lightly tap off the excess flour. Dip the cauliflower into the whisked eggs, ensuring they are completely coated, and let the excess drip off. Then place in the panko, pressing firmly to adhere.

4. Gently add the breaded cauliflower steaks into the hot oil, being careful that you are not overcrowding the pan. Fry until golden brown, 2 to 3 minutes. Flip and continue cooking for another 2 to 3 minutes, until crispy and golden on both sides. Remove the cauliflower to a wire rack set to drain excess oil and season with salt.

Make the Cabbage:

5. In a large bowl, mix together shredded cabbage and salt. Let sit for 2 minutes. Squeeze out the liquid from the cabbage and mix in the mayonnaise.

Build the Sandwiches:

6. Begin with a slice of milk bread, toasted side facing inside. Add a layer of cauliflower katsu, followed by tonkatsu sauce and cabbage. Top with the second slice of milk bread, toasted side facing inside. With a serrated knife, carefully cut off crust.

BROCCOLI CHEDDAR MELT

Makes 4 sandwiches
Prep Time: 15 minutes
Cook Time: 25 minutes

Nothing beats broccoli and cheddar. It's a classic combo if ever there was one, right up there with peanut butter and jelly and franks and beans. We take it a step further, melting mozzarella, cheddar, and American cheese into a sauce that coats the broccoli before we layer it between two more slices of cheddar, because you can't have too much cheese. It's simply not possible.

INGREDIENTS

Broccoli:
2 tablespoons neutral oil

1 large head broccoli, cut into medium florets

1 large head broccoli stems, grated

½ teaspoon kosher salt, plus more to taste

Ground black pepper

Cheese Sauce:
2 tablespoons unsalted butter

2 tablespoons all-purpose flour

1 cup whole milk

¼ cup shredded mozzarella cheese

¼ cup shredded sharp cheddar cheese

¼ cup torn American cheese (about 2 slices)

Sandwich Assembly:
8 slices sourdough bread

4 tablespoons (½ stick) unsalted butter, at room temperature

8 slices sharp cheddar cheese

INSTRUCTIONS

Cook the Broccoli:

1. Heat the neutral oil in a large sauté pan over medium heat until the oil is shimmering. Add the broccoli florets and shredded broccoli stems to the pan. Season with the salt and pepper and sauté for about 5 minutes, flipping occasionally, until slightly browned, tender, and vibrant green. Remove from the pan, wipe out the pan, and set aside.

Make the Cheese Sauce:

2. In a medium saucepan, melt the butter over medium heat then add the flour all at once. Cook and stir for 3 minutes so the butter and flour cook together, creating a roux.

3. Gradually stream in the milk while whisking to incorporate it completely into the flour mixture, creating a smooth consistency. While continuing to whisk, add the cheeses in increments until you have a smooth, thick sauce.

4. Turn off the heat and transfer the sautéed broccoli into the cheese sauce, folding gently until evenly incorporated. Cook together for a few minutes to ensure the mixture adheres well. Allow the mixture to cool slightly before assembling.

Cook the Sandwiches:

5. Place the pan used for cooking the broccoli back on medium heat to toast your sandwiches.

6. Spread softened butter on one side of the bread slices and lay the buttered side down in the pan.

7. Top each slice of bread with a cheddar cheese slice and then add a generous amount of the broccoli cheese filling to one half.

8. Once the cheddar slices have melted on the sourdough and the outside is golden brown, remove both halves and sandwich them together.

ALBERT NIAZHVINSKI'S WELLINGTON SANDO

Makes 2 sandwiches
Prep Time: 15 minutes
Cook Time: 30 minutes

We call this a Wellington sandwich, even though the main ingredient of a traditional Wellington—puff pastry—is missing. That's okay, because we have workarounds. When Albert Niazhvinski of *Albert Can Cook* made this for us on the *Idiot Sandwich* stage, he put a chopped-up croissant inside to mimic that classic puff pastry crunch. Our version uses crispy onions instead, because crispy onions make everything better. And since we clearly aren't paying attention to semantics here, if you want to add a side of beef broth and make it a dip, we won't stop you.

INGREDIENTS

Mushrooms:

3 tablespoons olive oil

1 pack (250 grams) mixed wild mushrooms or baby bella mushrooms, chopped into small pieces

½ to 1 tablespoon kosher salt

½ teaspoon freshly ground black pepper

1½ tablespoons fresh thyme leaves, chopped

1 croissant, rolled thin and julienned, optional

Rib Eye and Red Wine Pan Sauce:

2 tablespoons olive oil

Two 8-ounce rib eye or New York strip steaks

1 teaspoon kosher salt, plus more to taste

¼ teaspoon ground black pepper, plus more to taste

2 garlic cloves, smashed

2 thyme sprigs

2 tablespoons cold unsalted butter

3 tablespoons Dijon mustard

¼ cup red wine

½ cup beef stock

2 tablespoons cold unsalted butter, cubed

Sandwich Assembly:

1 small Italian loaf

Dijon Mayo (page 202), or substitute with store-bought

Crispy Onions (page 208), or substitute with store-bought fried onions

6 slices prosciutto, thinly sliced

INSTRUCTIONS

Cook the Mushrooms:

1. Heat a large skillet over medium heat and add the olive oil. Once shimmering, add the mushrooms and season with the salt and pepper. Add the thyme and cook, stirring constantly, until the mushrooms are deeply browned, about 20 minutes. Add the smashed croissant pieces, if using. Remove from the heat and reserve for assembly.

Cook the Steak:

2. Heat a large skillet over high heat and add the olive oil. Season the steak with the salt and pepper. Once the oil is shimmering, place the steaks in the skillet and cook until a crust forms, about 2 minutes. Flip the steaks and cook for another 2 minutes, then sear the edges for about 2 minutes each. Drop the heat to medium.

3. Add the garlic cloves and thyme sprigs. They will pop a little in the hot oil initially. Then add half of the cold butter and baste the steak until the internal temperature reaches 130°F, about 5 minutes, depending on the thickness of your steaks. Brush the steaks with the mustard, then remove from the pan, reserving the juices in the pan. Let the steak rest for at least 5 minutes, then slice against the grain into strips.

Make the Red Wine Pan Sauce:

4. In the same skillet used for the steaks, bring the heat back to medium-high and deglaze the pan with the red wine. Reduce the wine by three-quarters, then add the stock and reduce to about half. Whisk in the remaining cold butter and remove the garlic and thyme sprigs. Season with salt and pepper and reserve for assembly.

Build the Sandwiches:

5. Start by slathering both halves of the Italian loaf with Dijon Mayo. Add a layer of rib-eye slices, followed by mushrooms, a drizzle of the red wine pan sauce, and prosciutto slices. Top with Crispy Onions and the Italian loaf top. Cut the loaf into 2 sandwiches.

TONKATSU CUBANO

Makes 4 sandwiches
Prep Time: 15 minutes
Cook Time: 20 minutes

INGREDIENTS

Tonkatsu Sauce:

½ cup tonkatsu sauce (found in the Asian aisle)

1 tablespoon sriracha

½ teaspoon fresh lemon juice

Miso Mustard:

¼ cup white miso

¼ cup Dijon mustard

1 tablespoon honey

1 tablespoon rice wine vinegar

Tonkatsu:

1 to 2 cups neutral oil, for frying

1 cup all-purpose flour

2 teaspoons kosher salt, plus more for seasoning the cutlets

½ teaspoon ground black pepper, plus more for seasoning the cutlets

4 large eggs, whisked

1 cup panko breadcrumbs

4 pork cutlets, each ¼ to ½ inch thick

Sandwich Assembly:

4 Cuban loaves, cut in half lengthwise

4 tablespoons (½ stick) unsalted butter, softened, or nonstick cooking spray

12 slices deli ham

8 slices Swiss cheese

1 cup kimchi, with large, well-formed pieces

Technically, a Cubano is Cuban bread layered with sliced ham, roast pork, Swiss cheese, pickles, and tons of yellow mustard, then pressed to perfection under a hot plancha. We took that general idea and tonkatsu-ed it, because everything tastes better when it's breaded and fried.

INSTRUCTIONS

Make the Tonkatsu Sauce:

1. In a small bowl, whisk together tonkatsu sauce, sriracha, and lemon juice. Reserve for assembly.

Make the Miso Mustard:

2. In a small bowl, whisk together the miso, mustard, honey, and vinegar. Reserve for assembly.

Cook the Tonkatsu Pork:

3. Heat 2 inches of oil in a large skillet over medium heat to 350°F. Prepare three shallow dishes: Dish 1: Combine the flour, salt, and pepper; mix thoroughly. Dish 2: Whisk the eggs. Dish 3: Dump in the panko.

4. Season the pork cutlets with salt and pepper. Dip each cutlet into the flour mixture, then into the egg, and finally coat with the panko, pressing down to ensure even coverage. Cook each breaded cutlet in the hot oil for about 3 minutes on each side, until golden brown and the internal temperature reaches 145°F. Transfer the cooked cutlets to a wire rack to drain excess oil.

Cook the Sandwiches:

5. Preheat panini grill to 400°F, or use a nonstick pan with a heavy weighted press to substitute for the panini press.

6. Butter or spray the outside of the Cuban loaf halves. Spread miso mustard on the bottom half of the loaf, then layer in order with the tonkatsu pork, tonkatsu sauce, 3 slices of ham, 2 slices of cheese, and about ¼ cup kimchi.

7. Sandwich the two halves together and then grill and press in the panini grill for about 3 minutes, until the cheese has melted and the outside is golden brown.

CURRYWURST

Makes 4 sandwiches
Prep Time: 20 minutes
Cook Time: 45 minutes

INGREDIENTS

Caramelized Onions:

1½ tablespoons neutral oil

3 medium yellow onions, sliced

1 teaspoon kosher salt

¼ teaspoon ground black pepper

1 teaspoon sugar

Sausage Patties:

8 ounces raw pork sausage meat, or substitute raw pork breakfast sausage, or any well-seasoned bulk raw sausage mix

8 ounces ground beef, 80 percent lean

1 tablespoon whole grain mustard

1 tablespoon pilsner beer

2 tablespoons neutral oil

Sandwich Assembly:

12 ounces kielbasa sausage, sliced ¼ inch thick on a bias

4 seeded pretzel buns, sliced in half

Curry Ketchup (page 203)

When you think of Germany, curry probably doesn't immediately come to mind. But that's why we're writing this book, and you aren't, because curry happens to be the major ingredient in what is arguably Germany's most famous street food—currywurst. At its simplest, currywurst is ketchup mixed with curry powder plus a few other spices, then poured over a grilled sausage. Add some caramelized onions, a pretzel bun, and a DIY sausage patty with a little German pilsner mixed in, and you've got a bona fide *Idiot Sandwich* on your hands.

Caramelize the Onions:

1. Heat a large sauté pan over medium-high heat and add oil. Add the onions and cook until softened, about 5 minutes. Reduce the heat to medium-low and add the salt, pepper, and sugar. Cook for 20 to 30 minutes, stirring consistently, until the onions develop a deep caramel color. Set aside until ready to assemble.

Cook the Sausage Patties:

2. In a large bowl, combine the pork, beef, mustard, and pilsner. Mix until well incorporated. Form the mixture into 4 patties, each about 8 ounces and slightly wider than your pretzel buns.

3. Heat the neutral oil in a large skillet over medium-high heat. Place 4 patties in the hot pan and sear for 4 to 5 minutes. Flip the patties and sear the other side for another 4 to 5 minutes, until the internal temperature reaches 160°F and both sides are nicely caramelized. Remove the patties from the pan and set aside for assembly.

Sear the Kielbasa:

4. In the same pan, sear the kielbasa slices on both sides for 3 to 5 minutes, until golden brown and slightly crisp.

5. Set aside and toast your pretzel buns in the same pan.

Build the Sandwiches:

6. Spread Curry Ketchup on both halves of the pretzel bun. On the bottom half, add a sausage patty, followed by two to three kielbasa sausages and caramelized onions. Top with the other half of the pretzel bun.

PULLED PORK SLIDERS

Makes 12 sliders
Prep Time: 1 hour
Cook Time: 4½ hours

A pulled pork sandwich needs no introduction. Doing so would be the equivalent of introducing an alien to its mothership—they already know it exists, and it calls to them often. As for us, we'll never deny hunks of juicy pork piled high on a slider roll with crisp coleslaw, chipotle mayo, and tangy BBQ sauce. Resistance is futile. Beam us up already.

INGREDIENTS

Pulled Pork:

1 head garlic, peeled and chopped
3 tablespoons smoked paprika
2 tablespoons brown sugar
1 tablespoon fresh thyme leaves
1 teaspoon kosher salt
½ teaspoon ground black pepper
¼ cup olive oil
2 pounds boneless pork shoulder
3 white onions, peeled and quartered
8 thyme stems
1 cup chicken stock

Chipotle Mayo:

1 cup mayonnaise
4 teaspoons fresh lemon juice
1 tablespoon honey
2 tablespoons chopped chipotles in adobo
2 teaspoons whole grain mustard

Buttermilk Citrus Slaw:

½ cup buttermilk
¼ cup mayonnaise
Zest and juice of 1 lemon
1 tablespoon Dijon mustard
2 teaspoons apple cider vinegar
2 teaspoons honey
¼ head red cabbage, shredded
¼ head green cabbage, shredded
1 large carrot, peeled and grated

Sandwich Assembly:

12 slider buns, cut in half lengthwise and toasted
BBQ Sauce (page 199), or substitute with store-bought
Kosher salt
Ground black pepper

continued

INSTRUCTIONS

Roast the Pulled Pork:

1. In a large bowl, combine the garlic, paprika, brown sugar, thyme leaves, salt, pepper, and olive oil. Add the pork to the bowl and rub the marinade over the pork to cover completely. Let the pork marinate in the refrigerator for at least 1 hour or up to overnight.

2. Preheat the oven to 300°F. In a large roasting tray or heavy-bottom pot, layer the onions to cover the bottom completely. Add the thyme stems, then place the marinated pork over the onions and thyme. Pour the stock into the pot and cover with a lid. Roast the pork for 3½ to 4½ hours, until tender and easily pulled apart. Shred the pork, slice the onions, and combine with the cooking liquid. Set aside until ready to assemble the sandwich.

Make the Chipotle Mayo:

3. In a small bowl, combine mayonnaise, lemon juice, salt, pepper, honey, chipotles, and mustard. Refrigerate until ready to use.

Make the Buttermilk Citrus Slaw:

4. In a large bowl, combine the buttermilk, mayonnaise, lemon zest and juice, mustard, vinegar, and honey and season with salt and pepper. Whisk to combine. Add the shredded cabbage and grated carrots and toss to coat completely. Adjust the seasoning to taste and refrigerate until ready to use.

Build the Sandwiches:

5. Spread chipotle mayo on both halves of the slider bun. On the bottom half, layer pulled pork, followed by BBQ Sauce and buttermilk citrus slaw. Top with the other half of the slider bun.

NOTES FOR THE IDIOTS

Use store-bought pulled pork to save at least 3½ hours of cook time.

GRILLED EGGPLANT CAPONATA

Makes 4 sandwiches
Prep Time: 45 minutes
Cook Time: 40 minutes

We put raisins in this sandwich, and you probably think that's a mistake. Of course you do, because raisins are universally loathed by all humans. But wait until you eat one of the plump little buggers and realize they provide the perfect burst of moisture, sweetness, and texture. If you're a fan of weird-ass ingredients that create a sum much larger than its parts, then you are gonna adore the living daylights out of this sandwich.

INGREDIENTS

Red Pepper Pistou:

One 16-ounce jar roasted red bell peppers, drained

2 teaspoons fresh oregano leaves, chopped

6 tablespoons shredded Parmesan cheese

2 tablespoons extra-virgin olive oil

Eggplant Caponata:

1 to 2 large Italian eggplants, sliced lengthwise ¼ inch thick (10 to 12 slices)

4 teaspoons kosher salt

1 cup red wine vinegar or balsamic vinegar

⅓ cup sugar

¼ cup capers in brine, drained

¼ cup golden raisins, or substitute brown raisins

¼ cup finely diced celery

1 tablespoon orange zest

2 teaspoons red chile flakes

Neutral oil

Arugula Salad:

2 cups baby arugula

Juice of 1 lemon

Drizzle of extra-virgin olive oil

Sandwich Assembly:

¼ sheet focaccia, grilled

1 to 2 balls burrata cheese

Spiced Nuts (page 208)

Kosher salt

Ground black pepper

continued

INSTRUCTIONS

Make the Red Pepper Pistou:

1. In a food processor, combine the roasted red peppers, oregano, cheese, and olive oil and process until smooth, scraping the bowl with a rubber spatula as you go to ensure it's evenly combined. Season to taste with salt and pepper.

Cook the Eggplant Caponata:

2. Generously season both sides of the eggplant slices with salt and place them on paper towels or a resting rack over a sheet tray for 30 minutes to release excess water. This also removes the natural bitterness in the eggplant.

3. In a small saucepan, combine the vinegar, sugar, capers, raisins, celery, orange zest,and chile flakes. Bring to a simmer over low heat and simmer for 20 minutes, or until the mixture has reduced by half to three-quarters of the original volume and begins to thicken. Set aside to cool to room temperature.

4. Once the moisture has released from the eggplant, dab the eggplant slices with paper towels to dry. Place the eggplant in a bowl or zip-top bag and pour the reduced vinegar mixture over the slices, ensuring they are well coated. Let marinate for 15 minutes.

5. Brush a grill pan with neutral oil and heat over medium heat. Remove the eggplant from the marinade. Spoon out the veggie bits from the marinade and reserve for assembly. Lay the marinated eggplant on the grill pan without overcrowding. Cook until tender and lightly charred, 3 to 4 minutes per side. Remove the cooked eggplant from the grill and let it cool slightly.

Make the Arugula Salad:

6. In a small bowl, toss the arugula with the lemon juice and drizzle lightly with olive oil. Season lightly with salt and pepper. Sprinkle in the reserved veggie bits and fold together.

Build the Sandwiches:

7. Spread red pepper pistou on the bottom half of the focaccia. Layer on eggplant caponata, followed by torn burrata. Top with arugula salad, ensuring the veggie bits are evenly distributed, and sprinkle with Spiced Nuts. Finish with the top half of the focaccia.

PINEAPPLE JERK CHICKEN

Makes 2 sandwiches
Prep Time: 30 minutes
Cook Time: 20 minutes

Along with reggae and James Bond, jerk seasoning is probably the most famous invention to come out of Jamaica. And for good reason—it's shocking how flavorful jerked food can be, especially considering how easy it is to prepare. This sandwich is no different. Once you get all the spices, all you gotta do is marinate the chicken and throw it on the grill. And if you—like Gordon—are the type of idiot who likes pineapple on savory things like pizza, then you're in luck. We packed this sandwich full of them.

INGREDIENTS

Jerk Spice Blend and Chicken:

or substitute the spice blend with jerk seasoning

1 Scotch bonnet or habanero chile, seeds removed and chopped

1 tablespoon onion powder

1 tablespoon garlic powder

1 teaspoon ground allspice

1 tablespoon ground black pepper

2 teaspoons dried thyme

½ teaspoon ground nutmeg

1 tablespoon paprika

½ teaspoon ground ginger

½ teaspoon ground cinnamon

2 teaspoons kosher salt

¼ cup soy sauce

2 tablespoons molasses

Zest and juice of 1 medium orange

Zest and juice of 1 lime

1 tablespoon neutral oil, plus more for grilling

2 tablespoons brown sugar

Four 8-ounce chicken breast cutlets, patted dry

Grilled Pineapple:

4 rings fresh pineapple (¼ inch thick), or substitute with canned pineapple

Kosher salt

Slaw:

½ cup mayonnaise

1 tablespoon hot sauce

2 tablespoons pineapple juice or orange juice

2 tablespoons roughly chopped fresh parsley

2 cups shredded green cabbage

½ cup shredded carrot

3 tablespoons thinly sliced scallions

1 teaspoon kosher salt

Sandwich Assembly:

2 hoagie rolls, cut in half lengthwise and toasted

4 to 6 tablespoons mayonnaise or Spicy Cajun Mayo (page 201)

2 cups store-bought plantain chips

continued

INSTRUCTIONS

Cook the Jerk Chicken:

1. In a large bowl, combine the chiles, onion powder, garlic powder, allspice, pepper, thyme, nutmeg, paprika, ginger, and cinnamon and mix thoroughly. Add the salt, soy sauce, molasses, orange zest and juice, lime zest and juice, oil, and brown sugar. Add the chicken to the marinade, making sure the marinade is completely covering the chicken (keep it in the bowl or put it in a zip-top bag), and marinate for 30 minutes to 2 hours in the refrigerator.

2. Preheat a grill pan over high heat and brush with oil. Remove the chicken from the marinade and grill for about 3 minutes, until well browned. Flip and continue to grill on the other side until the chicken reaches an internal temperature of 160°F. Remove the chicken from the grill pan and set aside for assembly.

Grill the Pineapple and Get the Hoagie Rolls Ready:

3. Use the same grill pan as for the chicken. Brush the grill with neutral oil. Season the pineapple with salt and caramelize the pineapple pieces for about 4 minutes each side. Meanwhile, prepare the hoagie by lightly spreading mayonnaise on the inside and grilling until golden brown. Reserve for assembly.

Make the Slaw:

4. In a medium bowl, mix together the mayonnaise, hot sauce, and pineapple juice. Add the cabbage, carrots, parsley, and scallions to the mayonnaise mixture and toss to coat. Season with the salt. Reserve for assembly.

Build the Sandwiches:

5. Start with the bottom half of the hoagie bun and add two pieces of jerk chicken. Layer on grilled pineapple rings, followed by a generous amount of slaw and plantain chips. Top with the other half of the hoagie bun.

BRISKET SANDWICH

Makes 4 sandwiches
Prep Time: 20 minutes
Cook Time: 5½ to 6 hours

Not all brisket sandwiches are created equal, especially ones made in an oven, and ESPECIALLY ones coming from a British dude. Lucky for us, Gordon has a crackerjack team of recipe developers. Some of them are even from Texas, which is arguably the best place in the world for BBQ. They nailed it.

INGREDIENTS

Brisket:

3 to 3½ pounds brisket, ideally 1½ to 2 inches thick

2 tablespoons brown sugar

2 tablespoons sweet paprika or smoked paprika

2½ teaspoons onion powder

2 teaspoons dry mustard

2 teaspoons garlic powder

2 teaspoons kosher salt

¾ teaspoon ground cumin

¼ teaspoon cayenne pepper

1 teaspoon ground black pepper

Pickled Cucumbers:
or substitute with store-bought pickles

½ cup water

½ cup white wine vinegar

2 tablespoons sugar

¼ teaspoon kosher salt, plus more for salting the cucumber

2 Persian cucumbers or ½ English cucumber

Sandwich Assembly:

4 sesame buns, cut in half lengthwise, toasted

BBQ Sauce (page 199), or substitute with store-bought

Crispy Onions (page 208), or substitute with store-bought fried onions

INSTRUCTIONS

Cook the Brisket:

1. Score the brisket by making slits across the fat, being careful not to cut into the meat. In a small bowl, mix together the brown sugar, paprika, onion powder, dry mustard, garlic powder, salt, cumin, cayenne, and black pepper. Rub the spice mixture over all sides of the brisket, coating it well. Place the brisket in a 2-gallon zip-top bag or tightly wrap it in plastic wrap and let it marinate in the refrigerator for at least 4 hours or up to overnight.

2. Preheat the oven to 225°F. Place the spice rubbed brisket in a roasting pan and cover with a lid or seal tightly with aluminum foil. Roast for 5½ to 6 hours, until the meat is just about fork tender.

continued

3. Remove the foil and turn on the broiler. Broil until the outside of the brisket is browned. Remove from the oven and let the brisket rest for 20 to 30 minutes, then slice into ½-inch-thick pieces across the grain. Extra cooked brisket can be frozen for up to 1 month for sandwiches for another day.

Make the Pickled Cucumbers:

4. In a small pot, combine the water, vinegar, sugar, and salt. Place over medium heat and heat, stirring occasionally, until the sugar has dissolved. Remove from the heat and let the pickling liquid cool to room temperature.

5. Slice the cucumbers ¼ inch thick using a mandoline. Place in a large bowl, season lightly with salt, and let sit for 15 minutes to release excess liquid. Gently squeeze out the excess liquid and transfer the cucumbers to a jar or sealable container. Pour the pickling liquid over the cucumbers to cover and let marinate for at least 30 minutes or up to 1 hour.

Build the Sandwiches:

6. Start with the bottom half of the sesame bun and spread with BBQ Sauce. Add three to four slices of brisket, followed by pickles and Crispy Onions. Top with the sesame bun.

> **NOTES FOR THE IDIOTS**
> Use precooked BBQ brisket to save 5 hours or more of cooking time.

CHICKEN FRENCH DIP

Makes 4 sandwiches
Prep Time: 45 minutes
Cook Time: 2 hours

Now, we aren't saying we're geniuses for doing this (because we solely identify as idiots), but this sandwich is off the charts good, and OF COURSE IT IS because using a rich, slow-braised chicken stock as the jus for a French dip is just plain brilliant. Add some fall-off-the-bone chicken and an ungodly amount of caramelized onions, and you may never go back to your old beefy dips again.

INGREDIENTS

Braised Chicken and Jus:

3 tablespoons all-purpose flour

1 tablespoon kosher salt, plus more to taste

1 teaspoon ground black pepper, plus more to taste

½ teaspoon paprika

2 pounds bone-in chicken legs and thighs

3 tablespoons unsalted butter

1½ cups sliced white onion

4 garlic cloves

2 celery stalks, chopped

1 large carrot, chopped

4 cups chicken broth

2 tablespoons Worcestershire sauce

8 thyme sprigs or 1½ teaspoons dried thyme

4 tablespoons (½ stick) unsalted butter

French-Style Caramelized Onions:

1½ tablespoons extra-virgin olive oil

3 medium yellow onions, sliced

1 tablespoon sherry vinegar

1 tablespoon fresh thyme leaves, chopped

½ teaspoon kosher salt

¼ teaspoon ground black pepper

Sandwich Assembly:

4 hoagie rolls

12 slices provolone cheese

> **NOTES FOR THE IDIOTS**
>
> If you don't have a panini press, toast the sandwich in a pan and use a spatula to press it down manually.

continued

INSTRUCTIONS

Braise the Chicken:

1. Preheat a large Dutch oven or pot with a lid over medium heat. In a large bowl, mix together the flour, salt, pepper, and paprika and dredge the chicken pieces completely in the spice mixture.

2. Melt the butter in the pot, then, working in batches, add the chicken pieces and brown them on all sides, about 2 minutes per side. Remove the browned chicken pieces from the pot and set aside; repeat until all the chicken is browned.

3. Add the onion, garlic, celery, and carrot to the pot. Sauté until lightly browned, 10 to 15 minutes. Return the browned chicken to the pot along with the chicken stock, Worcestershire sauce, and thyme. Bring to a simmer. Cover with the lid and braise for 1 hour. Turn off the heat and let the chicken cool in the braising liquid.

4. Once cool enough to handle, remove the chicken from the liquid and shred it into large chunks, discarding the bones and skin. Strain the liquid and return to the stovetop over medium-high heat. Reduce the liquid by half to three-quarters the original volume and season with salt and pepper.

5. When ready to assemble the sandwiches, return the shredded chicken to the pot and pour enough reserved liquid over it to submerge the meat. Keep warm over medium-low heat. Reserve the remaining liquid for serving on the side for dipping the sandwiches later.

Caramelize the Onions:

6. Heat a large sauté pan over medium-high heat and add the olive oil. Add the sliced onions and cook until softened, about 5 minutes. Reduce the heat to medium-low and cook, stirring consistently, for 20 to 30 minutes, until the onions have a deep caramel color. Adding a small amount of water as the onions begin to brown will help caramelize the onions evenly. You can start your crusted brioche while the onions continue to cook and caramelize.

7. Add the vinegar, thyme, salt, and pepper and cook until the vinegar dissipates, about 5 minutes. Taste and adjust the seasonings.

Cook the Sandwiches:

8. Preheat a panini grill to 400°F.

9. Build a hoagie roll starting on the bottom half of the roll: Add a pile of the shredded chicken, 3 slices of cheese, and about ¼ cup of caramelized onions, then place the top of the hoagie roll on top and press the two halves together.

10. Spray the grill with cooking spray and press your sandwich for 2 to 4 minutes, until the top is crusted and the cheese has melted. Repeat to build the remaining sandwiches. Serve with warm jus for dipping.

ITALIAN BEEF

Makes 6 sandwiches
Prep Time: 30 minutes
Cook Time: 6 hours

Italian beef is a sandwich that has graced the streets of Chicago since the early 1900s, but it was a fairly well-kept secret until a certain television show came out in 2022 about a chef with piercing blue eyes, chiseled cheekbones, and an affinity for Calvin Klein. NO, not Gordon. The *other* one. There are countless variations, but pretty much all of them include thinly sliced beef on a hoagie roll with some sort of veggie garnish, usually giardiniera or peppers. We add a red pepper pistou to ours, which is decidedly not a classic Italian beef move, but it does kick it up a notch, which decidedly IS a classic *Idiot Sandwich* move.

INGREDIENTS

Roast Beef:
One 4-pound boneless beef chuck roast, 1½ to 2 inches thick

Spice Rub:
½ teaspoon garlic powder

1 teaspoon onion powder

3 tablespoons kosher salt

4 teaspoons ground black pepper

2 tablespoons Italian seasoning

4 teaspoons paprika

1 teaspoon red chile flakes

Braising Liquid:
¼ cup vegetable oil

1 cup chopped yellow onion

8 large garlic cloves, chopped

½ cup chopped celery

½ cup chopped carrots

6 to 8 cups beef broth

2 bay leaves

8 parsley sprigs

Red Pepper Pistou:
8-ounce jar roasted red bell peppers, drained

2 teaspoons fresh oregano leaves

6 tablespoons shredded Parmesan cheese

2 tablespoons extra-virgin olive oil

Sandwich Assembly:
6 Italian hoagie rolls, cut in half lengthwise and warmed

Sliced sweet or hot peppers, optional

Giardiniera (page 214), or substitute with store-bought

18 slices provolone cheese

Kosher salt

Ground black pepper

continued

INSTRUCTIONS

Cook the Roast Beef:

1. Preheat the oven to 300°F. In a small bowl, mix together the garlic powder, onion powder, salt, pepper, Italian seasoning, paprika, and chile flakes. Season the beef by pressing the spice mixture into the meat, ensuring it is well coated on all sides.

2. Heat an 8-quart Dutch oven or roasting pan over medium-high heat. Add the vegetable oil to coat the bottom of the pan. When nearly smoking, add the seasoned beef and sear for 2 to 3 minutes per side, until deeply golden brown and caramelized. Add the onion, garlic, celery, and carrots to the pan and lightly caramelize the vegetables.

3. Pour beef stock about three-quarters of the way to the top of your beef to nearly submerge the meat. Add the bay leaves and parsley sprigs. Bring to a boil, then reduce the heat to low. Cover with a lid or, if using a roasting pan, cover with foil. Transfer to the oven and braise for 5 to 6 hours, until the meat is tender.

4. Remove the beef from the oven and let cool enough so that the meat can be handled and remove from the braising liquid. Thinly slice the beef against the grain. Strain and discard the vegetables from the braising liquid and add the liquid to a large pan over medium heat. Once the liquid reaches just a simmer, place the sliced beef back in the warm braising liquid to keep it moist until ready to serve.

5. For the best flavor, make this a day in advance and let the meat chill in the liquid overnight until ready to use. Before assembly, make sure your meat is piping hot, so the cheese softens and melts when assembled.

Make the Red Pepper Pistou:

6. In a food processor or blender, combine the roasted red peppers, oregano, cheese, and olive oil and process until smooth. Season to taste with salt and pepper.

Build the Sandwiches:

7. Spread red pepper pistou on the bottom half of the hoagie roll. Layer on roast beef, followed by three slices of provolone cheese (you can warm the meat in a pan and melt the cheese before adding it to the sandwich). Top with Giardiniera and sweet or hot peppers, if desired, then place the top half of the hoagie roll on top.

> **NOTES FOR THE IDIOTS**
> Use store-bought braised roast beef to save over 5 hours of cook time.

CROQUE MONSIEUR

Makes 4 sandwiches
Prep Time: 15 minutes
Cook Time: 30 minutes

INGREDIENTS

Cheese Sauce:

4 tablespoons (½ stick) unsalted butter

¼ cup all-purpose flour

2 cups whole milk

½ cup grated Gruyère cheese

⅛ teaspoon ground nutmeg, optional

Pinch of kosher salt

Sandwich Assembly:

8 slices sourdough bread

4 tablespoons Dijon mustard

8 slices Gruyère or Swiss cheese

4 tablespoons (½ stick) unsalted butter

20 ounces ham, preferably French ham, thinly sliced

1 cup shredded Parmesan cheese

> **NOTES FOR THE IDIOTS**
>
> Use leftover cheese sauce to make mac and cheese or smother some tots or fries with it. The sauce can be stored in an airtight container for up to 5 days and warmed gently over medium heat.

The croque monsieur originated in the cafés of Paris during the 1910s. The name roughly translates to "mister crunch," but these sammies are so full of creamy, buttery, hammy goodness, a better name for them might actually be "mister gout." Ironically, the French word for *snack* is "goûter," so this works out great for everyone. Croque goûter it is. Use the best French ham you can find for optimal results.

INSTRUCTIONS

Make the Cheese Sauce:

1. In a medium saucepan, melt the butter over low heat, then add the flour all at once. Cook, stirring constantly, for 3 minutes to create a roux. Gradually stream in the milk while whisking to incorporate it completely into the flour mixture, creating a smooth consistency. While whisking, add the cheese in increments, along with nutmeg, if using, until the sauce is smooth and thick. Season to taste with salt. Turn off the heat and keep warm for assembly.

Cook the Sandwiches:

2. Preheat the broiler to high. In a medium skillet, melt the butter over medium to medium-high heat.

3. Spread mustard on the inner sides of 2 slices of sourdough bread. Top each slice with 2 slices of Gruyère cheese to cover the bread. Put the ham on top of the cheese on one of the slices and top with the other cheese-topped slice of bread.

4. Place the sandwich in the skillet and cook for 3 to 5 minutes per side, until golden brown. Transfer the sandwich to a lined baking tray. Repeat to make the remaining sandwiches.

5. Slather a thick layer of cheese sauce on top of the sandwiches. Sprinkle with the Parmesan cheese. Broil for 5 to 10 minutes, until the tops are golden and bubbling.

STEAK AND CHIMICHURRI

Makes 4 sandwiches
Prep Time: 15 minutes
Cook Time: 10 minutes

INGREDIENTS

Blue Cheese Aioli:

¾ cup mayonnaise

1 teaspoon minced garlic

3 tablespoons blue cheese crumbles

¼ teaspoon kosher salt

1 tablespoon fresh lemon juice

1 tablespoon buttermilk or whole milk

Skirt Steak:

20-ounce skirt steak

2 tablespoons oil from Chimichurri (page 195) or neutral oil

1½ to 2 teaspoons kosher salt

Sandwich Assembly:

12- to 18-inch baguette, sliced in half lengthwise and grilled

4 tablespoons blue cheese crumbles

Crispy Shoestring Potatoes (page 205), or substitute with store-bought crispy shoestring potatoes from the chip aisle

Chimichurri (page 195)

Chimichurri is an Argentinian sauce most often used as a condiment for grilled meats and fish. It's very similar to chermoula (page 113), except the spices are a bit different and it has the addition of red wine vinegar. We like to think we've mastered the steak sandwich with this one. The shoestring fries bring the crunch, the chimichurri brings the flavor, and the steak brings, well, the steak. Make the chimichurri in advance for a quick bite on a long night.

INSTRUCTIONS

Make the Blue Cheese Aioli:

1. In a food processor, combine the mayonnaise, garlic, blue cheese crumbles, salt, lemon juice, and buttermilk and process until smooth. Scrape the sides with a rubber spatula to ensure all ingredients are combined evenly.

Grill the Skirt Steak:

2. Preheat a grill pan or large sauté pan over high heat. Rub the chimichurri oil on the steak and season with the salt. Place the steak on the hot pan and cook for 2 to 5 minutes to caramelize.

3. Flip the steak and caramelize and cook the steak for another 2 to 5 minutes. Cook until the internal temperature reaches 120°F, or until desired doneness. Remove the steak and let it rest for 5 to 10 minutes, before slicing into thin strips.

Build the Sandwiches:

4. Start by spreading the bottom half of the baguette with blue cheese aioli. Layer on steak slices, followed by Chimichurri sauce, blue cheese crumbles, and Crispy Shoestring Potatoes, then finish with the baguette top.

PERI-PERI CHICKEN

Makes 4 sandwiches
Prep Time: 30 minutes
Cook Time: 45 minutes

INGREDIENTS

Peri-Peri Jam:

¼ cup olive oil

18 ounces cherry tomatoes

3 shallots, thinly sliced

3 tablespoons sliced fresh ginger (2-inch piece)

2 tablespoons peri-peri hot sauce

2 tablespoons honey

1 teaspoon kosher salt

⅓ teaspoon ground black pepper

Chicken and Rub:

3 tablespoons paprika

1 tablespoon dried oregano

2 tablespoons ground coriander

1 tablespoon kosher salt

2 teaspoons ground black pepper

½ teaspoon ground cardamom

2 tablespoons fresh lime juice

2 tablespoons neutral oil

1 tablespoon honey

8 boneless chicken thighs

Sandwich Assembly:

4 bolillo rolls or Portuguese rolls, warmed

Crispy Shoestring Potatoes (page 205)

Pil-pil, pili-pili, piri-piri, peri-peri, or African bird's eye—a pepper by any other name might be as hot, but it probably wouldn't make a chicken dish this tasty. The Portuguese introduced the peri-peri pepper to the countries of Southern Africa in the sixteenth century as they cruised around the continent trying to make a buck in the pepper trade. Later, they added olive oil, lemon juice, and vinegar and slathered it on a bird. Now, you will continue the legacy by layering that bird with some shoestring sweet potatoes in a nice hunk of crusty bread. Tchau-tchau!

INSTRUCTIONS

Make the Peri-Peri Jam:

1. In a small saucepan, heat the olive oil over medium heat. Once the oil is shimmering, add the cherry tomatoes, shallot, and ginger and cook until the tomatoes begin to burst, about 8 minutes. Add the peri-peri sauce and honey and continue cooking until thickened, about 15 minutes. Add the salt and pepper and bring the jam to room temperature before assembly.

Cook the Chicken:

2. Preheat the oven to 400°F. Line a sheet tray with parchment paper. In a small bowl, mix the paprika, oregano, coriander, salt, black pepper, and cardamom and rub the chicken thighs with the dry rub to coat. In the same bowl, mix in the lime juice, oil, and honey and pour over the spice-rubbed chicken either in a bowl or large zip-top bag, making sure all the chicken is evenly coated. Marinate for 30 minutes.

3. Place the chicken on the lined sheet tray skin side up. Place on the middle rack of the oven and roast for 10 minutes, or until the internal temperature of the meat is 160°F. Turn the oven to broil and continue to cook until the chicken skin is crispy, 3 to 5 minutes, rotating frequently as needed for even browning. Remove and let rest until assembly.

Build the Sandwiches:

4. Start with the bottom half of the bolillo roll and spread with peri-peri jam. Add two pieces of chicken thighs, followed by another layer of peri-peri jam. Top with Crispy Shoestring Potatoes and the bolillo roll top.

JOSH SCHERER'S CARNE ASADA CHEESESTEAK

Makes 2 sandwiches
Prep Time: 30 minutes
Cook Time: 20 minutes

Why choose one genre of tastiness when you can make two and fuse them into an epic sandwich of mythical proportions. That's what Josh Scherer of *Mythical Kitchen* did with his mash-up of carne asada and Philly cheesesteak. Not quite asada, not quite cheesesteak, but still somehow very much both, this sandwich is a true chimera. Josh used a sesame seed hoagie for his, but you could use a plain one if you prefer.

INGREDIENTS

Habanero Pickled Onions:

1½ cups white wine vinegar

1 habanero chile, seeds removed, thinly sliced

2 sprigs oregano

2 teaspoons kosher salt

1 large white onion, thinly sliced

Chipotle Cheese Sauce:

2 tablespoons unsalted butter

2 tablespoons all-purpose flour

1 cup whole milk

¼ cup shredded sharp cheddar cheese

¼ cup American cheese, torn (about 2 slices)

2 chipotles in adobo, finely chopped

Steak:

1 teaspoon dark chili powder

1 teaspoon garlic powder

1 teaspoon ground cumin

1½ teaspoons kosher salt, plus more to taste

½ teaspoon ground black pepper, plus more to taste

One 16-ounce rib eye steak, sliced into thin strips

2 tablespoons olive oil

1 poblano chile, sliced

1 small white onion, sliced

Sandwich Assembly:

Two 6-inch sesame hoagies, sliced open (hinge cut)

Picked cilantro leaves

1 lime, cut into wedges

continued

INSTRUCTIONS

Make the Habanero Pickled Onions:

1. In a small pot, combine the vinegar, habanero chile, oregano, and salt. Place over medium heat and heat, whisking until the salt dissolves. Place the sliced onions in a heatproof bowl. Pour the vinegar mixture over the onions and let cool to room temperature.

Make the Chipotle Cheese Sauce:

2. In a medium saucepan, melt the butter over low heat and add the flour all at once. Cook and stir the flour and butter mixture together for about 2 minutes to create a roux. Gradually stream in the milk, whisking to create a smooth consistency. Continue whisking while adding the cheeses in increments until a smooth, thick sauce forms. Fold in the chopped chipotle chile, then turn off the heat and reserve for assembly.

Cook the Steak, Poblano, and Onion:

3. Slice the steak into thin strips (freeze for 20 minutes before slicing for easier cuts). In a small bowl, combine the chili powder, garlic powder, cumin, salt, and pepper. Toss the steak slices in the spice mixture, ensuring they are well coated.

4. Preheat a large skillet over medium-high heat. Add the olive oil to the pan, then add the poblanos and onions. Season with salt and pepper. Cook until caramelized, about 5 minutes, then season again with salt and pepper.

5. Push the peppers and onions to one side of the pan and add the seasoned steak. Cook the steak for about 3 minutes on each side, until caramelized and cooked to your desired temperature.

Build the Sandwiches:

6. Start with the bottom half of the sesame hoagie roll and layer on the steak, poblano, and onion mix. Drizzle with chipotle cheese sauce, then add the habanero pickled onions and cilantro. Top with the sesame hoagie roll and serve with lime wedges.

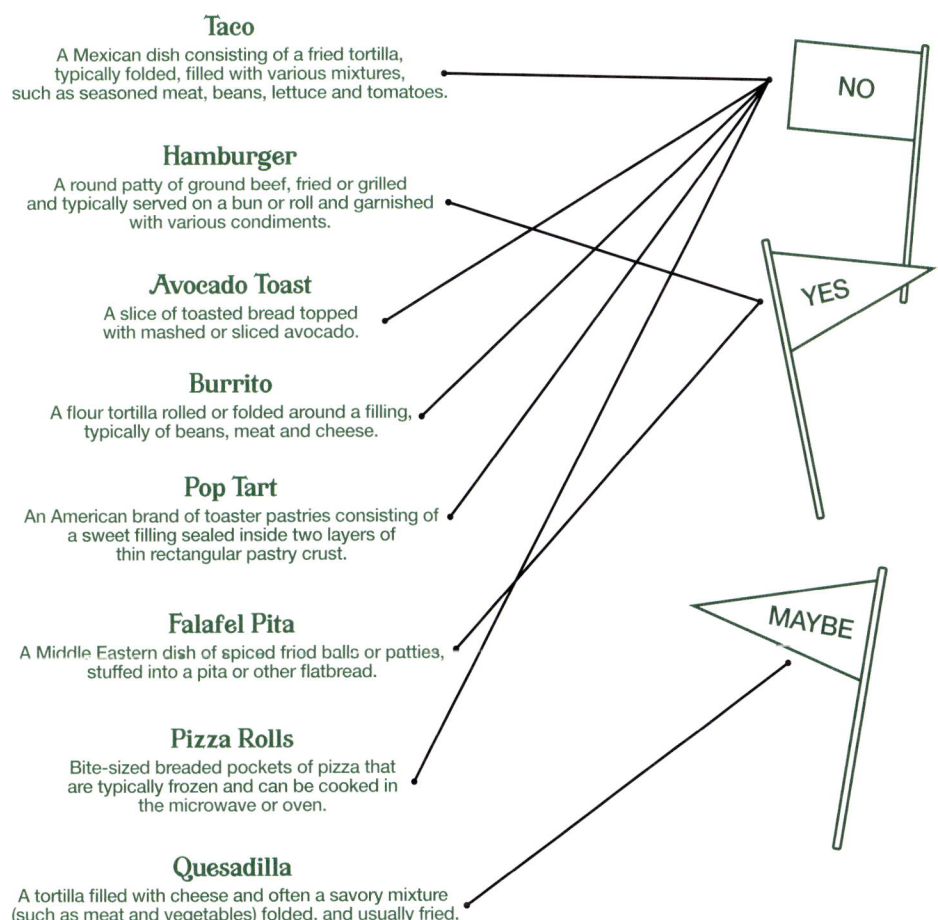

 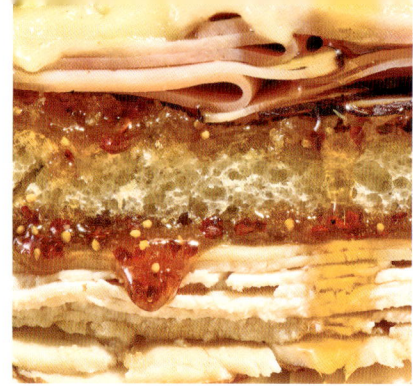  

SWEET

It's easy to assume there aren't a ton of options when it comes to sweet sandwiches beyond the classic ice cream sandwich or maybe an oatmeal crème pie. Lucky for you, where some might see a challenge, we saw untapped potential. All we had to do was reimagine the definition of "bread." And boy, did we get freaky. Griddled poundcake? BOOM. It's bread. Pressed sugar donuts?—Bread. Toasted stroopwafel and chewy oatmeal cookies—you guessed it. Bread. If you take nothing else from this book, know that anything can be a sandwich. All it takes is two or more slices of "bread" or a split roll and a delicious filling. Please refer to page 159 if you disagree.

Of course, this chapter is for all the sweet-toothed idiots out there, but we also included some sandwiches that err on the side of savory. The Triple-Decker Monte Cristo (page 183) and Sumac Strawberry (page 181) hit just the right balance.

Fruit Sando   163

Miso Sesame   165

Hazelnut Chocolate Panini   167

Chocolate Peanut Butter Whoopie Ice Cream Pie   168

Oatmeal Peaches and Crème Pie   171

PB&J Stuffed Toast   173

Stroopwafel S'mores   175

Coconut Alfajores   176

Banana Bread Sandwich   178

Sumac Strawberry and Sweet Labneh   181

Triple-Decker Monte Cristo   183

Cinnamon Apple Grilled Cheese   185

Blueberry and Lemon Curd Pound Cake Sandwich   186

Brioche and Espresso   189

Chocolate Cherry on Sourdough   190

FRUIT SANDO

Makes 4 sandwiches
Prep Time: 40 minutes
Cook Time: 10 minutes

INGREDIENTS

Yuzu Chantilly Cream:

6 tablespoons granulated sugar

2 tablespoons water

4 tablespoons yuzu juice, or substitute with concentrated mandarin orange juice

1 pint heavy cream

1 teaspoon vanilla extract

Sandwich Assembly:

8 slices milk bread (½ inch thick)

1 pint fresh strawberries, hulled and halved

1 mandarin orange, cut into segments, pith and membrane removed, or substitute with any orange variety or canned mandarins

2 kiwis, peeled and quartered lengthwise

NOTES FOR THE IDIOTS

The fruit needs to be laid out on paper towels to drain excess moisture, making it easier and cleaner for assembly.

Japan, you've done it again! Just when we thought you couldn't beat the egg salad sando (page 81), you came along and threw some fruit and whipped cream between two slices of milk bread and stole our hearts. Please accept our ode to you, this version of your famous fruit sando. We added some yuzu to the whipped cream because we like to keep you guessing.

INSTRUCTIONS

Make the Yuzu Chantilly Cream:

1. In a small pot, combine granulated sugar, water, and yuzu juice and place over medium heat. Bring to a boil, then reduce the heat to maintain a simmer and cook for 5 minutes to make a yuzu syrup. Remove from the heat and chill the syrup completely.

2. Pour the heavy cream into a stand mixer with a whisk attachment. Whip the cream at medium-low speed until soft peaks form.

3. Slowly stream in the cooled yuzu syrup while continuing to whip, then add the vanilla. Raise the speed to medium-high and whip until medium-firm peaks form. Be careful to not overwhip. Chill until ready for assembly.

Build the Sandwiches:

4. Spread 2 to 3 tablespoons of yuzu Chantilly cream across 4 slices of the milk bread.

5. Place 3 strawberry halves in a line down the center of the bread, from top to bottom.

6. Arrange about 3 mandarin orange slices in a line on one side of the strawberries.

7. Place 2 kiwi quarter slices in a line on the other side of the strawberries.

8. Spread 2 to 3 tablespoons of yuzu Chantilly cream on the top of the remaining 4 slices of milk bread.

9. Wrap the sandwiches in plastic wrap and chill for 30 minutes.

10. Using a serrated knife, trim off the crusts from all sides, then slice the sandwiches diagonally to reveal the fruit inside.

MISO SESAME

Makes 4 sandwiches
Prep Time: 10 minutes
Cook Time: 10 minutes

INGREDIENTS

Miso Caramel Sauce:

½ cup dark brown sugar

4 tablespoons (½ stick) unsalted butter

2 tablespoons heavy cream

1 tablespoon white miso

Donut Buns:

Nonstick cooking spray or unsalted butter

8 sugar-dusted yeast donuts

Sandwich Assembly:

1 pint black sesame ice cream

Toasted black sesame seeds

NOTES FOR THE IDIOTS

If you can't find black sesame ice cream, stir 3 tablespoons store-bought black sesame paste into vanilla ice cream or make your own black sesame paste by grinding 1 cup black sesame seeds with ½ teaspoon honey in a food processor.

You'll never look at a donut the same way after this. It'll start small. You'll see a jar of peanut butter and think, "Hey, you know what could be great is if I smash some donuts and make a PB&J with them." From there, you'll graduate to stranger fillings, things like melted marshmallows, chocolate custard, or even smoked deli meats. Your friends will start to look at you funny. There will be whispers of an intervention. No one will understand, until you make them this sandwich.

INSTRUCTIONS

Make the Miso Caramel Sauce:

1. In a small saucepan, combine the brown sugar, butter, heavy cream, and miso.
2. Heat over medium heat, whisking, for 3 to 5 minutes, until the sugar melts completely and the mixture coats the back of a spoon well. Allow to cool to room temperature before assembly.

Toast the Donut Buns:

3. Using a rolling pin, flatten the donuts to about ¼ inch thick.
4. Heat a griddle or sauté pan over medium heat and spray with cooking spray to lightly coat the pan. Add the flattened donuts to the pan.
5. Place a piece of parchment paper over the donuts and weigh them down with a cast-iron pan or another heavy object for 45 seconds to 1 minute while they caramelize so they maintain their thickness.
6. Remove the weight and parchment, then flip the donuts and cook the second side for 1 to 3 minutes, until golden brown and crispy. Allow the donuts to cool completely before assembly.

Build the Sandwiches:

7. Using an ice cream scoop or spoon, place a generous amount of ice cream on one flattened donut.
8. Add the top flattened donut and press the two together gently. The ice cream should spread to the edges of the donuts.
9. Place the assembled sandwich in the freezer for at least 30 minutes to firm.
10. Remove from the freezer and drizzle with miso caramel, then sprinkle with toasted black sesame seeds.

HAZELNUT CHOCOLATE PANINI

Makes 4 paninis
Prep Time: 5 minutes
Cook Time: 10 minutes

INGREDIENTS

Salted Caramel Sauce:

or substitute with store-bought caramel sauce

½ cup dark brown sugar

2 tablespoons unsalted butter

2 tablespoons heavy cream

Chantilly Cream:

1 cup heavy cream

3 tablespoons granulated sugar

1 teaspoon vanilla extract

Sandwich Assembly:

4 slices ciabatta bread, cut ¼ inch thick

2 tablespoons unsalted butter, softened

6 tablespoons Nutella or other hazelnut chocolate spread

1 bar (3.5 ounces) of chocolate

2 tablespoons toasted and chopped hazelnuts

Flaked sea salt

Sometimes it's the basic things that taste the best. Take this sandwich, for example. It's made of two common ingredients—salted caramel and Nutella—then pressed into a panini for the sweet sandwich mash-up you didn't know you wanted. Hand us one of these, steam up a pumpkin spice latte, and throw some Uggs on our cold little feet, because if being basic is wrong, we don't want to be right.

INSTRUCTIONS

Make the Salted Caramel Sauce:

1. In a small saucepan, combine the brown sugar, butter, and heavy cream. Place over medium heat and bring to a simmer.
2. Whisking continuously, keep cooking until the sugar has dissolved and the sauce coats the back of a spoon. Cool to room temperature before assembly.

Make the Chantilly Cream:

3. Pour the heavy cream into a stand mixer fitted with a whisk attachment.
4. Whip the cream at medium speed until soft peaks form. Slowly add the granulated sugar until fully incorporated. Add the vanilla and raise the speed to medium-high. Continue whipping until medium-firm peaks form, being careful not to overwhip.

Cook and Build the Sandwiches:

5. Preheat a panini machine to 400°F.
6. Spread softened butter on the outside of the ciabatta slices and spread Nutella on the inside of the ciabatta slices.
7. Press the ciabatta in the panini grill and cook for about 3 minutes, until the outside is nicely toasted. Remove from the grill and drizzle with the caramel sauce and sprinkle with a small pinch of flaked salt.
8. Top with the Chantilly cream. Use a Microplane to grate the chocolate bar over the top and finish with a sprinkle of hazelnuts.

CHOCOLATE PEANUT BUTTER WHOOPIE ICE CREAM PIE

Makes 20 whoopie pies

Prep Time: 2 hours

Cook Time: 15 minutes

Whoopie pies, also known as moon pies, are a beloved American dessert. Not a cookie, or a cake, or even a pie, these strangely named confections are perfect vehicles for ice cream. This is one case where it's absolutely worth the trouble of making the ice cream from scratch—we've provided a scrumptious, wildly easy, no churn recipe. But you can also purchase chocolate peanut butter ice cream from the grocery store. It will still be delicious, we promise.

INGREDIENTS

Chocolate Peanut Butter Fudge Ice Cream:

One 14-ounce can sweetened condensed milk

½ cup cocoa powder

1 teaspoon vanilla extract or vanilla bean paste

Pinch of kosher salt

2 cups heavy cream

½ cup thick fudge sauce, at room temperature

½ cup peanut butter chips

Whoopie Pie Cookies:

1⅔ cups all-purpose flour

⅔ cup Dutch-process cocoa powder

1½ teaspoons baking soda

½ teaspoon fine sea salt

½ cup (1 stick) unsalted butter, at cool room temperature

1 cup lightly packed dark brown sugar

1 large egg, at room temperature

1 teaspoon vanilla extract

1¼ cups buttermilk, at room temperature

INSTRUCTIONS

Make the Chocolate Peanut Butter Fudge Ice Cream:

1. Pre-chill a 9 x 5 x 3-inch loaf pan in the freezer. In a medium bowl, whisk the condensed milk, cocoa powder, vanilla, and salt.

2. In a stand mixer, whip the heavy cream on medium-high speed for about 2 minutes, until you have soft peaks. Fold one-third of the whipped cream into the condensed milk mixture, then gently fold in the rest. Pour into the chilled loaf pan and freeze for 2 hours.

3. Remove from the freezer and stir in fudge and peanut butter chips to create ribbons. Freeze for 3 more hours, or until firm and ready to assemble.

Make the Whoopie Pie Cookies:

4. Preheat the oven to 350°F. Line 2 sheet trays with parchment paper. In a medium bowl, sift the flour, cocoa powder, baking soda, and salt.

5. In a stand mixer with the paddle attachment, beat the butter and brown sugar on medium-high speed for 3 minutes, or until fluffy. Scrape the bowl using a rubber spatula as you go.

6. Add the egg and vanilla and beat for another 3 minutes. Alternate mixing in half the flour mixture and the buttermilk until combined. The batter should be thick and sticky. Chill for 30 minutes.

7. Scoop 1½-tablespoon mounds onto the prepared sheets, 2 inches apart. Bake for 9 to 10 minutes, until the tops look dry. Remove from the oven and let rest on the sheet tray for 5 minutes, then transfer to a wire rack to cool completely before assembling.

Build the Sandwiches:

8. Lay a whoopie pie cookie on a flat surface with the flat side facing up. Scoop a heaping amount of the chocolate peanut butter fudge ice cream and place it in the center of the cookie.
9. Place another whoopie pie cookie on top, flat side down. Gently press the top cookie down so the ice cream spreads evenly between the two cookies.
10. Place the assembled whoopie pies in the freezer and keep them there until ready to eat.

NOTES FOR THE IDIOTS

Want to save some time? Buy your favorite premade brand of peanut butter chocolate ice cream to substitute the homemade version. I'm not going to tell you that easier is better in this case, but do what you like!

OATMEAL PEACHES AND CRÈME PIE

Makes 15 pies
Prep Time: 30 minutes
Cook Time: 15 minutes

INGREDIENTS

Oatmeal Cookies:

2 cups all-purpose flour

1½ teaspoons ground cinnamon

1 teaspoon baking soda

1 teaspoon kosher salt

1 cup (2 sticks) unsalted butter, softened

1 cup granulated sugar

1 cup packed brown sugar

2 large eggs

1 teaspoon vanilla extract

3 cups quick-cooking oats

Nonstick cooking spray

Cream Cheese Filling:

8 ounces cream cheese, at room temperature

½ teaspoon vanilla bean paste or extract

1 cup powdered sugar

Sandwich Assembly:

One 13-ounce jar peach preserves

Picture this: a low-lit bar with red velvet seats and smooth jazz playing in the background. A woman in a large, brimmed hat takes a seat. She orders a dry martini with extra olives, then winks at the man on her right. Well, he's not a man, he's actually an anthropomorphized peach. And this is no ordinary woman, she's Little Debbie of Oatmeal Creme Pie fame, but she's all grown up. Long story short, she and the peach hit it off and they had a baby and you're about to eat the physical embodiment of their love.

INSTRUCTIONS:

Make the Oatmeal Cookies:

1. In a medium bowl, mix the flour, cinnamon, baking soda, and salt. In a stand mixer using the paddle attachment, beat the butter, granulated sugar, and brown sugar until light and fluffy, about 3 minutes. Scrape the sides of the bowl with a rubber spatula, ensuring it's evenly mixed. Add the eggs one at a time, then mix in the vanilla. Gradually add the flour mixture and then mix in the oats. Cover and chill the dough for at least 1 hour. Chilling prevents the cookies from spreading too much as they bake.

2. Preheat the oven to 350°F and line 2 sheet trays with parchment paper or spray with nonstick cooking spray. Scoop the dough into 1- to 1½-inch portions and place on the lined sheet trays about 2 inches apart. Bake for 8 to 10 minutes, rotating the trays halfway through. Bake until the edges are golden and the centers of the cookies are set. Remove the trays from the oven, cool the cookies on the sheet trays for 5 minutes, then transfer to a wire rack to finish cooling completely.

Make the Cream Cheese Filling:

3. In a stand mixer using a clean bowl and a paddle attachment, beat the cream cheese and vanilla until smooth and creamy. Gradually mix in the powdered sugar until fluffy. Place the frosting in a piping bag or zip-top bag (snip the end off just before piping) to pipe the cream cheese filling in assembly.

Build the Sandwiches:

4. Place two oatmeal cookies with the flat side facing up. Spread peach preserves on one and a layer of cream cheese filling (about ¼ inch thick) on the other. Gently sandwich the two cookies together.

PB&J STUFFED TOAST

Makes 4 sandwiches
Prep Time: 10 minutes
Cook Time: 30 minutes

INGREDIENTS

Strawberry Compote:

1 pound fresh strawberries, hulled and quartered, or substitute with frozen strawberries

2 tablespoons granulated sugar

¼ teaspoon kosher salt

1½ tablespoons fresh lemon juice

2 teaspoons cornstarch

Peanut Butter Honey Coating:

4 tablespoons (½ stick) unsalted butter, at room temperature

¼ cup light brown sugar

2 tablespoons honey

1 tablespoon creamy peanut butter

¼ teaspoon kosher salt

Sandwich Assembly:

1 brioche loaf

4 to 6 ounces creamy peanut butter

¼ cup honey-roasted peanuts, crushed

THE MORE YOU KNOW
(ABOUT SANDWICHES)

The average American will have consumed 1,500 PB&Js by the time they turn 18.

The best thing about this sandwich, besides the fact that it's slathered in peanut butter and honey on the outside, then caramelized to a deep, golden brown, is its versatility. Don't stop with just strawberry jam, because you could stuff any flavor in this baby. Bananas would be great, too—even marshmallows. This recipe is only as tasty as your imagination, so use it wisely.

INSTRUCTIONS

Make the Strawberry Compote:

1. In a medium pot, combine the strawberries, sugar, salt, and lemon juice. Place over medium heat and bring the mixture to a simmer. Cook for about 15 minutes, until the strawberries are tender but still hold their shape.

2. Remove about 2 tablespoons of the liquid from the cooking strawberries, and in a separate small bowl or cup, mix the cornstarch into the liquid to make a slurry. Whisk the slurry into the strawberries on the stovetop and cook for an additional minute, or until the compote thickens and becomes glossy. Remove from the heat and let cool to room temperature before assembly.

Make the Peanut Butter Honey Coating:

3. In a small bowl, mix together the butter, brown sugar, honey, peanut butter, and salt until well combined. Reserve the mixture for toasting.

Build the Sandwiches:

4. Preheat the oven to 350°F and line a sheet tray with parchment paper. Slice the brioche loaf into eight 2-inch-wide slices and trim the crusts off all sides. Use a paring knife to create a pocket by inserting it into the center of one end of each slice. Stuff each slice with 1 to 2 tablespoons peanut butter and 1 to 2 tablespoons strawberry compote.

5. Spread 2 tablespoons of the peanut butter honey coating on all sides of each stuffed brioche slice. Coat each piece completely in the crushed honey-roasted peanuts. Place the assembled slices on the lined sheet tray and bake for 10 minutes. Flip the toasts over and bake for an additional 8 to 10 minutes, until golden brown. Remove from the oven and let rest for 10 minutes before serving.

STROOPWAFEL S'MORES

Makes 4 sandwiches
Prep Time: 10 minutes
Cook Time: 10 minutes

INGREDIENTS

Ganache:

⅓ cup heavy cream

2 ounces milk chocolate or semi-dark chocolate chips or chopped bar

1 teaspoon vanilla extract

Sandwich Assembly:

4 jumbo marshmallows

8 honey stroopwafel cookies

2 tablespoons chopped pecans or another nut, optional

The only thing better than a regular s'more is one you don't have to build a fire to make. Enter this recipe. We went out on a limb and used stroopwafel cookies instead of graham crackers, traded the jumbo-sized marshmallows for the fluff, and transformed the humble chocolate bar into a creamy ganache, enabling you to make this sandwich ooey and gooey without a hint of an open flame. Now you're cooking with fire—metaphorically, of course.

INSTRUCTIONS

Make the Ganache:

1. Heat the heavy cream in a small saucepan over medium heat until it just begins to steam, being careful to not let it boil. Remove from the heat and add the chopped chocolate and vanilla extract. Whisk until the ganache is smooth and glossy. Transfer the ganache to a small bowl, cover, and refrigerate for at least 1 hour, until fully chilled.

2. Using a hand mixer, whip the chilled ganache for about 2 minutes, until light and fluffy. Use a rubber spatula to scrape down the sides of the bowl to ensure everything is evenly mixed.

3. Transfer the whipped ganache to a piping bag (or zip-top bag with one corner of the bag snipped to create an opening about ½ inch wide) in preparation for assembly.

Build the Sandwiches:

4. Preheat the oven to 400°F.

5. Lay 4 stroopwafels on a sheet tray. Top each with 1 marshmallow and toast in the oven or microwave for 3 to 5 minutes, until puffed and golden brown. Remove from the oven and set aside.

6. Pipe a ½-inch-wide ring of whipped ganache around the edge of each of the remaining stroopwafels. Gently press the two halves together, then roll in the chopped nuts, if using.

COCONUT ALFAJORES

Makes 10 to 12 sandwiches
Prep Time: 40 minutes
Cook Time: 10 minutes

The alfajores of Latin America are, at their most basic, crumbly butter cookies sandwiched together with dulce de leche and rolled in coconut. We forgo the traditional dulce de leche here and opt to go hard on the coconut, caramelizing coconut cream instead. There's no other way to say this . . . we're cuckoo for coconuts.

INGREDIENTS

Coconut Cream Filling:

One 14-ounce can unsweetened coconut cream

½ cup dark brown sugar

½ teaspoon kosher salt

¼ teaspoon baking soda

1 teaspoon vanilla bean paste or extract

Shortbread Cookies:

¾ cup unbleached all-purpose flour

¾ cup cornstarch

½ teaspoon baking powder

½ teaspoon kosher salt

½ cup (1 stick) unsalted butter, softened

¼ cup granulated sugar

2 large egg yolks

1 teaspoon vanilla bean paste or extract

Sandwich Assembly:

¼ cup unsweetened shredded coconut, toasted

INSTRUCTIONS

Make the Coconut Cream Filling:

1. In a large saucepan, combine the coconut cream, dark brown sugar, salt, vanilla, and baking soda. Place over medium-high heat and bring to a light boil. Cook, stirring occasionally, for 25 to 30 minutes, until the sauce is very thick. Set the coconut cream filling aside to cool. If the filling seems to separate, mix well with a fork or whisk to bring it back together before using.

Bake the Shortbread Cookies:

2. Preheat the oven to 350°F. Line 2 sheet trays with parchment paper. In a medium bowl, sift the flour, cornstarch, baking powder, and salt and set aside.

3. In the bowl of a stand mixer fitted with a paddle attachment, cream the butter and sugar on medium speed until light and fluffy. Scrape the bowl with a rubber spatula as it mixes to ensure it's all fully combined. Add the egg yolks one at a time, making sure each is fully incorporated before adding the next, then add the vanilla. Turn the speed down to low and gradually add the flour mixture until it just comes together.

4. On a clean, dry surface, turn the dough out of the bowl and knead it a few times by hand to ensure everything is well incorporated. Place the dough between two sheets of parchment paper to prevent sticking and roll the dough out to about ⅛ inch thick.

5. Using a 2-inch round cookie cutter, cut out 20 to 24 cookie halves, combining the scraps and re-rolling as necessary. Arrange the cookies on the prepared sheet trays, leaving at least ½ inch between each cookie.

6. Refrigerate the cookies on the trays for about 20 minutes (this prevents the dough from spreading too thin while baking). Once chilled, bake for 10 minutes, or until the cookies have puffed and are dry to the touch. Remove from the oven and let cool on the sheet tray for 5 minutes. Transfer the cookies to a wire rack to fully cool before assembly.

Build the Sandwiches:

7. Start with a shortbread cookie, then add a layer of coconut cream filling. Top with the second shortbread cookie and gently press the two together. Carefully roll the edges in shredded coconut so it sticks to the cream filling.

BANANA BREAD SANDWICH

Makes 6 sandwiches
Prep Time: 15 minutes
Cook Time: 1 hour 10 minutes

We remember some bits of 2020 fondly. Specifically, the parts where we got to make endless loaves of banana bread. And even though those times were top-tier bananas, it doesn't mean we have to stop making banana bread just because they're over. We've upped the ante by adding a cream cheese swirl, some caramel sauce, Chantilly cream, and even more bananas. Because you can take the idiot out of quarantine, but you can't take the quarantine out of the idiot.

INGREDIENTS

Banana Bread:
or substitute with store-bought banana bread

Nonstick cooking spray

3 cups mashed very ripe bananas

½ cup (1 stick) unsalted butter, melted

¾ cup packed dark brown sugar

1 large egg

2 teaspoons vanilla bean paste or extract

1 teaspoon baking soda

½ teaspoon kosher salt

1½ cups plus 3 tablespoons all-purpose flour

4 ounces cream cheese, at room temperature

¼ cup granulated sugar

Caramelized Bananas and Walnut Carmel Sauce:

2 tablespoons unsalted butter

4 large, firm bananas, cut in half lengthwise and widthwise (it's important to use firm bananas so they don't break down and get mushy as they cook)

¼ cup walnut pieces

1 cup brown sugar

2 teaspoons ground cinnamon

½ teaspoon ground nutmeg, optional

Pinch of kosher salt

½ cup heavy cream

Chantilly Cream:
or substitute with whipped cream topping

2 cups heavy cream

¼ cup granulated sugar

1 teaspoon vanilla bean paste or extract

INSTRUCTIONS

Make the Banana Bread:

1. Preheat the oven to 350°F. Coat an 8½ x 4- to 5-inch loaf pan with nonstick spray. Line the pan with two long strips of parchment paper: one for the length and one for the width to create "handles" for easy removal of the loaf after it is baked.

2. In a large bowl, combine the mashed bananas, melted butter, brown sugar, egg, vanilla, baking soda, and salt. Stir until combined. Mix in 1½ cups of the flour until incorporated, then set aside. In the bowl of a stand mixer fitted with a paddle attachment, beat the cream cheese and granulated sugar until smooth. Add the egg and vanilla to the cream cheese mixture and mix until smooth, scraping the sides as necessary. Sprinkle the remaining 3 tablespoons flour into the cream cheese mixture and mix until just combined.

3. Spread about half of the banana bread batter into the bottom of the prepared pan. Pour the cream cheese mixture over the batter, then spread the remaining banana bread batter on top. Bake for 50 to 60 minutes, until the center is set. Allow the bread to cool in the pan for about 20 minutes, then remove it carefully by pulling up on the parchment strips and lifting the loaf from the pan. Cool completely on a wire rack, at least 20 minutes, then cut into twelve 1-inch-thick slices.

Prepare the Caramelized Bananas and Walnut Caramel Sauce:

4. Heat a large sauté pan over medium-high heat and add butter. Lightly brown the butter, about 2 minutes. Add the banana slices to the pan in an even layer and cook to caramelize without moving them, 1 to 2 minutes. Flip each banana slice over and caramelize the other side, another 1 to 2 minutes. Add the walnuts and toast for about 1 minute. Stir in the brown sugar, cinnamon, nutmeg, and salt. When the sugar has fully melted, add the cream and stir until the caramel comes together. Remove from the heat and reserve for assembly.

Make the Chantilly Cream:

5. In a stand mixer fitted with a whisk attachment, whip the cream at medium speed until soft peaks form. Slowly add the sugar until fully incorporated. Add the vanilla and raise the speed to medium-high. Continue whipping until medium-firm peaks form, being careful not to overwhip. Use immediately or refrigerate until ready to use.

Build the Sandwiches:

6. Start with a slice of banana bread, then add a layer of caramelized bananas. Drizzle with walnut caramel sauce and top with Chantilly cream. Finish with the second slice of banana bread.

SUMAC STRAWBERRY AND SWEET LABNEH

Makes 4 sandwiches
Prep Time: 10 minutes
Cook Time: 10 minutes

Labneh is just as good sweet as it is savory, and you'll fully agree after tasting this. As for the raisin bread, we know it can be divisive, but it goes great with the sourness of the sumac strawberries. If we can't convince you, then go for a brioche toast instead. It's your world, we're just living in it.

INGREDIENTS

Sumac Strawberry Compote:

1 pound fresh strawberries, hulled and quartered

2 tablespoons granulated sugar

¼ teaspoon kosher salt

1½ teaspoons sumac

1½ tablespoons fresh lemon juice

2 teaspoons cornstarch

Sweet Labneh:

8 ounces labneh

2 tablespoons powdered sugar

Sandwich Assembly:

8 slices raisin bread, toasted

INSTRUCTIONS

Make the Sumac Strawberry Compote:

1. In a medium pot, combine the strawberries, sugar, salt, sumac, and lemon juice. Bring the mixture to a simmer over medium heat and cook for about 15 minutes, until the strawberries are tender but still hold their shape.

2. Remove about 2 tablespoons of the liquid from the cooking strawberries to a separate small bowl or cup and mix the cornstarch into the liquid to make a slurry. Whisk the slurry into the strawberries on the stovetop and cook for an additional minute until the compote thickens and becomes glossy. Remove from the heat and let cool to room temperature before assembly.

Make the Sweet Labneh:

3. In a small bowl, mix the labneh and powdered sugar until the sugar dissolves. Chill in the refrigerator until ready for assembly.

Build the Sandwiches:

4. Begin with a slice of raisin bread, then spread with sweet labneh. Add a layer of sumac strawberry compote and top with the second slice of raisin bread.

NOTES FOR THE IDIOTS

To save time, mix 1½ teaspoons sumac into a 15-ounce jar of store-bought strawberry jam instead of making the compote from scratch.

NOTES FOR THE IDIOTS

If you have leftover turkey from the holidays or the Turkey Breakfast Club sandwich (page 48), use it here.

TRIPLE-DECKER MONTE CRISTO

Makes 2 sandwiches
Prep Time: 30 minutes
Cook Time: 20 minutes

INGREDIENTS

Chile Fig Jam:
3 tablespoons fig jam

1¼ teaspoons Aleppo chile flakes

Sandwich Assembly:
6 slices white bread, cut at least ¼ inch thick

¼ cup Dijon Mayo (page 202)

4 slices Black Forest ham

4 slices oven-roasted turkey

8 ounces Brie cheese, sliced ¼ inch thick

2 tablespoons unsalted butter, at room temperature

Powdered sugar, for dusting

Maple syrup, optional

Batter:
2 large eggs

2 tablespoons milk

1 tablespoon granulated sugar

½ teaspoon vanilla extract

¼ teaspoon ground cinnamon

Pinch of ground nutmeg, optional

Pinch of kosher salt

Piled high with ham, turkey, and cheese, most idiots would think the Monte Cristo is a savory sandwich. We are not most idiots. When you consider the fact that this is chock-full of fig jam, battered, fried, and dusted with an obscene amount of powdered sugar, we wouldn't call it anything *other* than a sweet treat. And we do mean treat. Its decadence is unsurpassed (except by maybe the Croque Monsieur, page 151).

INSTRUCTIONS

Make the Chile Fig Jam:
1. Whisk the fig jam and chile flakes together until combined and set aside.

Build the Sandwiches:
2. Prepare the first layer by spreading mayonnaise on the first slice of bread. Add 2 slices of ham.
3. Prepare the second layer by spreading chile fig jam on one side of the second slice of bread. Place it chile fig jam–side down on the ham.
4. Spread more chile fig jam on the top of this slice. Add 2 slices of turkey and a layer of Brie cheese over the turkey.
5. Spread mayonnaise on the last slice of bread and place it mayo-side down to close the sandwich

Press the Sandwiches:
6. Cover the sandwiches with parchment or plastic wrap. Place a cast-iron skillet on top for 1 to 2 minutes to press and compact. This step helps make it easier to handle when you batter your sandwiches.

Prepare the Batter and Cook the Sandwiches:
7. Heat a skillet or griddle over medium-low heat. In a shallow dish, whisk the eggs, milk, sugar, vanilla, cinnamon, nutmeg, if using, and salt. Melt 2 tablespoons of butter into the skillet. Dip each sandwich in the batter and cook for 3 to 4 minutes per side, until golden brown and the cheese melts. Remove from the pan.
8. Slice each sandwich in half, dust with powdered sugar, and serve with additional chile fig jam or maple syrup.

CINNAMON APPLE GRILLED CHEESE

Makes 4 sandwiches

Prep Time: 10 minutes

Cook Time: 45 minutes

INGREDIENTS

Cinnamon Apple Compote:

3 large Granny Smith apples, peeled and diced

2½ teaspoons ground cinnamon

Pinch of ground nutmeg

¼ teaspoon kosher salt

2½ tablespoons fresh lemon juice

5 tablespoons light brown sugar

1 teaspoon vanilla extract

2 teaspoons cornstarch

Crispy Croissants:

8 croissants

6 tablespoons honey

3 tablespoons unsalted butter, softened

Sandwich Assembly:

12 ounces sharp white cheddar cheese, shredded

We couldn't possibly confine the brilliance of smashing a beautiful pastry, caramelizing it, and turning it into bread to *only* the Miso Sesame sandwich (page 165). In this case, we subbed the donut for a croissant and doused it in honey, but the general procedure stays the same. We smash, we toast, we taste. The only way this sandwich could be improved is if we added some sharp white cheddar and cinnamon-spiced apples, just like they do in the South. So, we did.

INSTRUCTIONS

Make the Cinnamon Apple Compote:

1. In a medium pot, combine the apples, cinnamon, nutmeg, salt, lemon juice, brown sugar, vanilla extract, and ½ cup water. Bring the mixture to a boil over medium heat, then reduce the heat and simmer for 20 minutes, or until the apples are tender but still hold their shape.

2. In a small bowl, mix the cornstarch with 2 tablespoons water to create a slurry. Add the slurry to the compote, stirring it in well. Cook for an additional 3 minutes, or until the compote is glossy and has thickened. Remove from the heat and set aside for assembly.

Cook and Build the Sandwiches:

3. Begin by making the crispy croissants. On a clean cutting board, use a rolling pin to flatten the croissants to about ¼ inch thickness.

4. In a small bowl, combine the honey and softened butter, then slather it on each side of the pressed croissants.

5. Heat a large griddle pan over medium heat. Place 2 croissants on the pan. Place a piece of parchment on the croissants and place a cast-iron pan (or similar heavy item) over them to weight them. Press down for 45 seconds to 1 minute.

6. Remove the weight and parchment, then flip the croissants. Put the cheese on top and cook for an additional 1 to 3 minutes, until the bottom is golden brown and crispy and the cheese has melted.

7. Remove the pressed croissants from the pan and spread the apple compote evenly on top of the cheese. Top with the second smashed croissant and repeat with the remaining croissants to make the rest of the sandwiches.

BLUEBERRY AND LEMON CURD POUND CAKE SANDWICH

Makes 6 sandwiches
Prep Time: 25 minutes
Cook Time: 1 hour 40 minutes

INGREDIENTS

Pound Cake:
¾ cup (1½ sticks) unsalted butter, at room temperature

1½ cups granulated sugar

3 large eggs, at room temperature

1 teaspoon pure vanilla extract

1½ cups all-purpose flour

¼ teaspoon baking powder

¼ teaspoon kosher salt

¾ cup whole milk

Blueberry Crème Fraîche:
½ cup good-quality store-bought blueberry jam

1½ cups crème fraîche

1 tablespoon lemon zest

Sandwich Assembly:
Nonstick cooking spray or unsalted butter

1 cup store-bought lemon curd

½ cup fresh blueberries

Powdered sugar, for dusting

There's nothing not to love about fresh blueberries, lemon curd, and crème fraîche smothering griddled slices of pound cake. Plus, this sandwich is so easy to make, you probably could have it done in the time it takes you to read this intro, especially if you go the lazy route and buy all the ingredients from the grocery store instead of making them from scratch. Are you done making it yet??

INSTRUCTIONS

Make the Pound Cake:

1. Preheat the oven to 325°F. Line an 8½ x 4- to 5-inch loaf pan with two long strips of parchment paper, creating "handles" for easy removal. In a stand mixer, cream the butter and sugar for about 5 minutes on medium speed, until light and fluffy. Use a rubber spatula to scrape the sides of the bowl to ensure it is mixed evenly. Slowly add the eggs one at a time, ensuring each is well mixed before adding the next. Mix in the vanilla with the last egg.

2. In a separate bowl, sift together flour, baking powder, and salt. Add half of the flour mixture to the creamed butter and mix well. Add half of the milk and mix just until combined. Add the remaining flour mixture, then the remaining milk, incorporating it completely.

3. Pour the batter into the prepared loaf pan and bake for 50 to 60 minutes, until a skewer or toothpick inserted into the center comes out clean. Allow the cake to cool for at least 30 minutes before removing it from the pan by lifting the parchment paper handles. Cool for another 20 minutes before cutting into ½-inch slices.

Make the Blueberry Crème Fraîche:

4. Put the crème fraîche in a small bowl. Add dollops of blueberry jam and lemon zest and lightly fold to create a marbled effect. Reserve in the refrigerator until ready for assembly.

Toast the Pound Cake:

5. Heat a griddle or large nonstick skillet over medium heat. Lightly spray with cooking spray or butter. Carefully place the pound cake slices on the hot griddle and toast for 2 to 3 minutes until golden brown on one side only. Remove from the griddle and reserve.

Build the Sandwiches

6. Start with the toasted side facing down and spread with lemon curd. Top with the second slice of pound cake, griddled side up. Add a dollop of blueberry crème fraîche, a few fresh blueberries, and dust with powdered sugar.

NOTES FOR THE IDIOTS

Using store-bought pound cake will save you an hour and a half of cook time.

BRIOCHE AND ESPRESSO

Makes 4 sandwiches
Prep Time: 15 minutes

INGREDIENTS

Espresso Whipped Cream:

1 cup heavy cream

6 tablespoons powdered sugar, sifted

2 tablespoons instant espresso powder

Sandwich Assembly:

Dinner roll sized soft brioche buns

¼ cup shelled pistachios, chopped

This sandwich is reminiscent of a giant cream puff, but without all the extra work of making pâte à choux from scratch. In fact, we did the math and can show that this recipe achieves the optimal exertion ratio of 75 percent less work to 100 percent more flavor. The secret is hollowing out the brioche to make room for more of that tasty espresso whipped cream.

INSTRUCTIONS

Make the Espresso Whipped Cream:

1. Whip the cream in a stand mixer on medium speed until soft peaks form, 3 to 5 minutes. Add the powdered sugar and espresso powder; mix to combine. Continue whipping on medium speed until stiff peaks form, 2 to 4 minutes. Set aside.

   Alternate method for a stronger espresso whipped cream:

   Mix the instant espresso with the cream and let steep in the refrigerator for 2 to 3 hours, then continue whipping as instructed above.

Build the Sandwiches:

2. Cut a slit in the center of each brioche bun, about one-third to halfway down. Slice at an angle on both sides of the slit to remove a small wedge. Scoop out a little more bread to create space for the filling.

3. Using a spoon or spatula, fill the center of the brioche bun with espresso whipped cream and spread it evenly so that it lines up seamlessly with the bun, about ¼ cup per roll. Serve immediately or store in an airtight container in the fridge for up to 1 day. When ready to serve, top the espresso cream with chopped pistachios.

CHOCOLATE CHERRY ON SOURDOUGH

Makes 4 sandwiches
Prep Time: 10 minutes
Cook Time: 15 minutes

We took all the great parts about a box of chocolates and turned them into a sandwich: creamy filling, tart, sugary cherries, and rich dark chocolate, all on toasted sourdough. The result is actually pretty similar to a Black Forest cake—but better, because it's a sandwich.

INGREDIENTS

Cherry Compote:
or substitute with a good-quality store-bought cherry compote

12 ounces frozen dark sweet cherries

1½ tablespoons granulated sugar

1½ teaspoons fresh lemon juice

Pinch of kosher salt

1½ teaspoons cornstarch

Sweet Mascarpone Spread:

4 ounces mascarpone cheese, softened

3 ounces cream cheese, softened

2 tablespoons powdered sugar

Sandwich Assembly:

8 slices sourdough bread, ¼ inch thick

One 1½- to 2-ounce dark chocolate bar, broken into pieces

6 tablespoons unsalted butter, softened

INSTRUCTIONS

Make the Cherry Compote:

1. In a medium pot, combine the cherries, sugar, lemon juice, and salt. Bring to a boil over medium heat, then reduce the heat and simmer for 10 minutes.

2. In a small bowl, mix the cornstarch with 2 tablespoons water to create a slurry. Whisk the slurry into the compote and mix well. Cook for 1 minute, or until the compote is glossy and thickened. Remove from the heat and cool for assembly.

Make the Sweet Mascarpone Spread:

3. In a small bowl, mix the mascarpone cheese, cream cheese, and powdered sugar using a rubber spatula until fully combined. Chill completely in the refrigerator or in the freezer for about 15 minutes. Chilling will prevent the mixture from melting too quickly when you toast the sandwiches.

Cook the Sandwiches:

4. Heat a griddle over medium heat.

5. Butter one side of each sourdough slice and lay the slices butter side down on a clean surface. Then spread 2 to 3 tablespoons of cherry compote on the other side of one slice of bread and sprinkle chocolate bar pieces into the compote. Spread 3 to 4 tablespoons sweet mascarpone spread on the other slice of bread.

6. Place the sandwich on the griddle and toast the outsides until golden brown, about 2 to 3 minutes per side.

CONDIMENTS

Let's be honest, it's the condiments that make the sandwich. Imagine eating a BLT with no mayonnaise. Or a meatball sub with no marinara. Classic sides make great toppings as well—if you've never put potato chips on a sandwich, then you've never lived. Really, anything can be a condiment when you put your mind to it. So go ahead, clean out your fridge. Yesterday's cold fries will be perfect. Just ask our good friend the Chip Butty (page 79).

The condiments on the pages that follow, while not day-old fries, will take your sandwiches to the next level. You'll find them in many of the recipes throughout this book, but don't stop with what we tell you to do—mix and match these babies. Throw Crispy Onions (page 208) on a random sandwich for some crunch. Drizzle your grilled cheese with chili oil and drown your bologna in Garlic Sauce (page 195). Have a little fun—we won't mind. We already said this in the intro, but in case you missed it: If you need to save some time and energy, we fully support you buying your condiments premade from the store, when applicable. These recipes will be here waiting for you when you have the bandwidth to make them.

SPREADS AND SAUCES

Avocado Green Goddess   194

Buttermilk Ranch   194

Chimichurri   195

Garlic Sauce   195

Horseradish Cream Cheese   196

Salsa Verde   196

Coriander Chutney   197

Spicy Tomato and Mushroom Chutney   198

Whipped Feta   198

BBQ Sauce   199

Pesto   199

AVOCADO GREEN GODDESS

Used in Fish, No Chips (page 99).

Makes 1½ cups   Prep Time: 10 minutes

INGREDIENTS

2 garlic cloves

½ teaspoon Dijon mustard

½ cup mayonnaise

½ teaspoon white wine vinegar

½ cup watercress, or substitute with arugula or spinach

1½ tablespoons fresh tarragon leaves, chopped

1½ tablespoons chopped fresh chives

1½ tablespoons chopped fresh parsley leaves

1½ tablespoons shredded Parmesan cheese

1 tablespoon fresh lemon juice

½ cup sour cream or plain Greek yogurt

1 cup diced avocado (about 1 small avocado)

Kosher salt to taste

½ teaspoon cayenne pepper

INSTRUCTIONS

1. Combine all the ingredients in a food processor or blender and process until smooth. Use a rubber spatula to scrape the sides to make sure it's blended completely and thoroughly. Add salt to taste and adjust the consistency with water as needed. Store in an airtight container in the refrigerator for up to 1 week.

BUTTERMILK RANCH

Used in Blackened Salmon (page 117).

Makes 1¾ cups   Prep Time: 5 minutes

INGREDIENTS

½ cup sour cream

½ cup buttermilk

½ cup mayonnaise

1 teaspoon kosher salt

¼ teaspoon ground black pepper

¼ teaspoon garlic powder

2 tablespoons thinly sliced fresh chives

3 tablespoons chopped fresh dill

3 tablespoons fresh parsley, chopped

2 teaspoons dry mustard powder

1 teaspoon fresh lemon juice

A few dashes of hot sauce, optional

INSTRUCTIONS

1. In a medium bowl, whisk all the ingredients until well incorporated. Chill before use or store in an airtight container in the refrigerator for up to 1 week.

CHIMICHURRI

Used in Steak and Chimichurri (page 153).

Makes 1½ cups   Prep Time: 10 minutes

INGREDIENTS

¼ cup red wine vinegar

3 small garlic cloves, minced

⅔ cup fresh chopped parsley leaves

3 tablespoons minced shallots

¼ cup chopped fresh cilantro

1 tablespoon dried oregano

½ teaspoon red chile flakes

1 teaspoon kosher salt

¼ teaspoon ground black pepper

1 cup neutral oil

INSTRUCTIONS

1. In a small bowl, combine the vinegar, garlic, parsley, shallots, cilantro, oregano, chile flakes, salt, and pepper and mix until well incorporated. Whisk in the oil and add salt to taste. Store in an airtight container in the refrigerator for up to 3 days.

GARLIC SAUCE

Used in Falafel Pita (page 95) and Kofta Pita (page 118).

Makes 1 cup   Prep Time: 5 minutes   Cook Time: 10 minutes

Be sure to use fresh garlic, not the peeled, packaged kind. It does *not* taste the same. And don't skip the milk blanching step—it removes the extra bite from the garlic, making the sauce extra smooth.

INGREDIENTS

1 cup milk

⅔ cup garlic cloves

3 tablespoons fresh lemon juice

Kosher salt

¾ cup neutral oil

INSTRUCTIONS

1. In a small pot, combine the milk and garlic cloves. Bring to a simmer over medium heat, then lower the heat and continue to simmer for 10 minutes.
2. Use a slotted spoon to remove the garlic and place it in a food processor. Add the lemon juice to the processor and process until it forms a rough paste.
3. Slowly add the neutral oil through the hole in the lid while processing until the mixture becomes smooth. Season with salt to taste. Store in an airtight container in the refrigerator for up to 5 days.

HORSERADISH CREAM CHEESE

Used in Pastrami Egg and Cheese (page 51) and Whitefish Salad Sandwich (page 19).

Makes ½ cup   Prep Time: 5 minutes

INGREDIENTS

- 4 ounces cream cheese, at room temperature
- 1 tablespoon prepared horseradish
- 1 tablespoon thinly sliced fresh chives
- ¼ teaspoon kosher salt, plus more to taste
- ¼ teaspoon freshly cracked black pepper

INSTRUCTIONS

1. In a small bowl, mix the cream cheese, horseradish, chives, salt, and pepper. Store in an airtight container in the refrigerator for up to 5 days.

SALSA VERDE

Used in Chilaquiles Torta (page 20) and Achiote Pork (page 120).

Makes 2 cups   Prep Time: 10 minutes   Cook Time: 10 minutes

INGREDIENTS

- 1 pound tomatillos, husks removed
- ½ small white onion, quartered
- 1 serrano chile (add a second for more kick)
- 2 large garlic cloves
- 2 teaspoons chicken bouillon powder, optional
- 1 bunch roughly chopped cilantro, including the tender stems
- 2 teaspoons Mexican oregano
- Kosher salt

INSTRUCTIONS

1. Fill a medium pot with water and bring to a simmer over medium-high heat. Add the tomatillos, onion, and chile. Cook for about 5 minutes, until tender. Drain, reserving ½ cup of the cooking liquid, and transfer to a blender.
2. Add the garlic, chicken bouillon, cilantro, oregano, and salt to taste to the blender. Blend until smooth, thinning with the reserved water if necessary and scraping the sides of the blender with a rubber spatula as needed so that it is evenly blended. Add salt to taste and store in an airtight container in the refrigerator for up to 5 days.

CORIANDER CHUTNEY

Used in Mumbai Masala Toast (page 14).

Makes 2 cups   Prep Time: 5 minutes

INGREDIENTS

2 tablespoons chopped jalapeño chiles (seeds removed for less spice)

¼ cup roasted unsalted peanuts

3 large garlic cloves

2½ teaspoons peeled and chopped fresh ginger

1 teaspoon cumin seeds

¼ teaspoon ground turmeric

Juice of 1 lime

2 bunches roughly chopped cilantro including stems

1 to 1½ teaspoons kosher salt

INSTRUCTIONS

1. In a blender or food processor, combine the chiles, peanuts, garlic, ginger, cumin seeds, turmeric, and lime juice. Blend until you have a coarse paste.
2. Add the cilantro, 2 tablespoons of water, and the salt and continue blending until you reach a smooth paste consistency. Taste and adjust the seasoning as needed. Store in an airtight container in the refrigerator for up to 4 days.

SPICY TOMATO AND MUSHROOM CHUTNEY

Used in Short Rib Toastie (page 108).

Makes 1½ to 2 cups Prep Time: 5 minutes Cook Time: 20 minutes

INGREDIENTS

1 tablespoon olive oil

4 ounces sliced mixed mushrooms or baby portobellos

1 tablespoon seeded and minced jalapeño chile

4 ounces cherry tomatoes

1 shallot, thinly sliced

1-inch piece fresh ginger, peeled and minced

1 teaspoon kosher salt

¼ teaspoon ground black pepper

1 tablespoon honey

INSTRUCTIONS

1. In a large skillet, heat the olive oil over medium heat. When the oil is shimmering, add the mushrooms and cook, stirring, until browned, about 10 minutes.
2. Add the chile and cook until softened, about 3 minutes. Add the cherry tomatoes, shallot, and ginger. Season with the salt and pepper and cook until the tomatoes begin to burst, about 5 minutes.
3. Stir in the honey and continue cooking until thickened, about 5 minutes. Adjust the seasoning with salt and pepper to taste. Store in an airtight container in the refrigerator for up to 5 days.

WHIPPED FETA

Used in Shakshuka Sandwich (page 35) and Braised Lamb and Feta (page 113).

Makes about ½ cup Prep Time: 5 minutes

INGREDIENTS

4 ounces feta cheese

¼ cup plain Greek yogurt

Zest of 1 lemon

1 tablespoon extra-virgin olive oil

INSTRUCTIONS

1. In a food processor, combine the cheese, yogurt, and lemon zest. Process until light, fluffy, and smooth. Drizzle in the olive oil through the top of the processor until combined. Use a rubber spatula to scrape the sides of the processor so that it is evenly blended. Store in an airtight container in the refrigerator for up to 1 week.

BBQ SAUCE

Used in Pulled Pork Sliders (page 132) and Brisket Sandwich (page 141).

Makes 1 cup   Prep Time: 5 minutes   Cook Time: 20 minutes

INGREDIENTS

- 2 tablespoons neutral oil
- 1 tablespoon onion powder
- 8 large garlic cloves, minced
- Kosher salt
- Ground black pepper
- 6 tablespoons brown sugar
- 2 tablespoons smoked paprika
- ½ cup cider vinegar
- ½ cup ketchup
- 8 teaspoons Worcestershire sauce

INSTRUCTIONS

1. Heat the neutral oil in a medium saucepan over medium heat. Once shimmering, add the onion powder, garlic cloves, a pinch of salt and pepper, brown sugar, and paprika. Cook until the sugar melts and the paprika is fragrant, 2 to 4 minutes.
2. Stir in the vinegar, ketchup, and Worcestershire sauce. Bring to a boil, then reduce the heat to maintain a simmer. Cook until thickened and syrupy, about 20 minutes. Store in an airtight container in the refrigerator for up to 1 week.

PESTO

Used in Green Eggs and Ham (page 27) and Susi Vidal's Spicy Chicken Parm (page 59).

Makes 1 cup   Prep Time: 10 minutes

INGREDIENTS

- ¼ cup pine nuts, toasted
- 2 small garlic cloves
- ¾ cup shredded Parmesan cheese
- 2 cups (3 ounces) fresh basil leaves
- 2 tablespoons fresh lemon juice
- ½ cup extra-virgin olive oil
- ½ teaspoon red chile flakes or minced jalapeño, optional
- Kosher salt

INSTRUCTIONS

1. In a food processor, combine the toasted pine nuts, garlic, and cheese. Process until roughly chopped. Add the basil, lemon juice, olive oil, and chile flakes, if you're making a spicy pesto.
2. Pulse until the mixture is evenly combined. Scrape the sides of the bowl with a rubber spatula to evenly combine the ingredients. Season with salt and adjust the thickness by adding more oil, if needed. Store in an airtight container in the refrigerator for up to 4 days.

MAYOS

Not all mayonnaise is created equal—some have MSG, some add vinegar, others use whole eggs, and some use just the yolks. All of them are delicious, so unless we call out a specific brand to use, find one you like and stick with that. From there, you can use the recipes below to inspire your next creation, mixing mayonnaise with any spice or saucy thing you like. Chili crisp mayo, garlic sauce mayo, chimichurri mayo—the possibilities are endless, and you'll look like a culinary genius.

Spicy Cajun Mayo   201

Basil Mayo   201

Dijon Mayo   202

Whole Grain Mustard Mayo   202

SPICY CAJUN MAYO

Used in Cajun Breakfast Sandwich (page 3).

Makes ¼ cup   Prep Time: 5 minutes

INGREDIENTS

¼ cup mayonnaise

2 teaspoons fresh lemon juice

2 teaspoons Old Bay Seasoning

1 tablespoon hot sauce, preferably Crystal brand

Pinch of kosher salt, plus more to taste

INSTRUCTIONS

1. In a medium bowl, combine the mayonnaise, lemon juice, Old Bay Seasoning, hot sauce, and salt. Taste and adjust the salt as needed. Store in an airtight container in the refrigerator for up to 1 week.

BASIL MAYO

Used in Turkey Breakfast Club (page 48).

Makes 1 cup   Prep Time: 5 minutes

INGREDIENTS

1 cup mayonnaise

4 teaspoons fresh lemon juice

1½ cups packed fresh basil leaves

Pinch of kosher salt, plus more to taste

INSTRUCTIONS

1. In a food processor, combine the mayonnaise, lemon juice, basil leaves, and salt. Scrape sides of food processor to blend thoroughly. Taste and adjust the salt to taste. Store in an airtight container in the refrigerator for up to 4 days.

DIJON MAYO

Used in Triple-Decker Monte Cristo (page 183) and Albert Niazhvinski's Wellington Sando (page 126).

Makes 1 cup   Prep Time: 5 minutes

INGREDIENTS

1 cup mayonnaise

3 tablespoons Dijon mustard

Pinch of kosher salt

Pinch of ground black pepper

INSTRUCTIONS

1. In a small bowl, mix the mayonnaise, mustard, salt, and pepper thoroughly until combined. Store in an airtight container in the refrigerator for up to 1 week.

WHOLE GRAIN MUSTARD MAYO

Used in French Onion Omelet Sandwich (page 16) and Pork Belly (page 55).

Makes 1 cup   Prep Time: 10 minutes

INGREDIENTS

1 cup mayonnaise

6 tablespoons stone-ground mustard

1 tablespoon finely chopped fresh parsley leaves

2 teaspoons thinly sliced fresh chives

Zest and juice of ½ lemon

Kosher salt

Ground black pepper

INSTRUCTIONS

1. In a small bowl, combine the mayonnaise, mustard, parsley, chives, and lemon zest and juice and stir to combine thoroughly. Season with salt and pepper. Store in an airtight container in the refrigerator for up to 1 week.

KETCHUPS

Curry Ketchup 203

Spicy Ketchup 203

CURRY KETCHUP

Used in Currywurst (page 131).

Makes 1 cup   Prep Time: 5 minutes

INGREDIENTS

¾ cup tomato ketchup

4 teaspoons curry powder

1 tablespoon sweet paprika

2 teaspoons Worcestershire sauce

2 teaspoons honey

1 teaspoon chili powder

Pinch of kosher salt, plus more to taste

INSTRUCTIONS

1. In a small bowl, whisk the ketchup, curry powder, paprika, Worcestershire sauce, honey, chili powder, and salt. Add salt to taste and store in an airtight container in the refrigerator for up to 1 week.

SPICY KETCHUP

Used in Hong Kong–Style Egg Sandwich (page 32) and Chip Butty (page 79).

Makes ½ cup   Prep Time: 2 minutes

INGREDIENTS

½ cup ketchup

3 tablespoons gochujang (Korean chile paste) or hot sauce, or to taste

INSTRUCTIONS

1. In a small bowl, whisk the ketchup and gochujang well and set aside. To make the ketchup spicier, add more gochujang or hot sauce to taste. Store in an airtight container in the refrigerator for up to 1 week.

CRISPY AND CRUNCHY

Chili Crisp   205

Crispy Shoestring Potatoes   205

Hot Honey Bacon   206

Crispy Wontons   207

Crispy Prosciutto   207

Spiced Nuts   208

Crispy Onions   208

Parm Frico   209

Crispy Garlic   210

CHILI CRISP

Used in Onigirazu: A Japanese Sushi Sandwich (page 93).

Makes 1 cup   Prep Time: 10 minutes   Cook Time: 45 minutes

INGREDIENTS

1 cup neutral oil

2 cups minced shallots or white onion

¼ cup minced garlic

2 teaspoons peeled and minced fresh ginger

2 tablespoons soy sauce

¼ cup red chile flakes

1 tablespoon togarashi with sesame seeds

1 teaspoon kosher salt, or to taste

INSTRUCTIONS

1. In a small sauce pot, combine the oil and shallots. Bring to a simmer over medium-low heat, stirring occasionally, for 35 to 45 minutes, until the shallots are golden brown and starting to crisp.
2. Reduce the heat to low, add the garlic and ginger, and cook until the garlic is amber colored and crispy, about 5 minutes. Remove from the heat and let cool for 1 minute. Add the soy sauce, red chile flakes, togarashi, and salt and mix well to combine. Store in an airtight container in the refrigerator for up to 1 week.

CRISPY SHOESTRING POTATOES

Used in Steak and Chimichurri (page 153) and Peri-Peri Chicken (page 155).

Makes 1 quart   Prep Time: 10 minutes   Cook Time: 10 minutes

INGREDIENTS

1 large sweet potato or russet potato

1 quart neutral oil, for frying

Kosher salt

INSTRUCTIONS

1. In a countertop fryer or large pot, heat the oil over medium-high heat to 350°F. Peel the sweet potato and thinly julienne it lengthwise using a mandoline or knife.
2. Fry small batches of shredded potatoes for about 5 minutes, stirring frequently, until they are golden brown and crispy. Use a slotted spoon or spider to remove the sweet potatoes as they are done and drain on a plate or sheet tray lined with paper towels. Season with salt and store in an airtight container at room temperature for up to 3 days.

HOT HONEY BACON

Used in Fried Green BLT Sliders (page 73) and Chili Spiced French Toast Sandwich (page 7).

Makes 6 slices   Prep Time: 5 minutes   Cook Time: 20 minutes

INGREDIENTS

3 tablespoons honey

¼ teaspoon cayenne pepper

Pinch of ground ancho chile powder, or chile powder of choice

6 slices bacon

INSTRUCTIONS

1. Preheat the oven to 350°F. Line a sheet tray with parchment paper. In a small saucepan, mix the honey, cayenne, and chile powder and heat over low heat for 3 to 5 minutes so the spices and honey combine.
2. Lay the bacon on the prepared sheet tray in a single layer, brush with the hot honey mixture, and bake for 10 minutes.
3. Carefully remove the tray from the oven, flip the bacon, and brush with the remaining honey mixture. Return the pan to the oven and bake for another 5 to 10 minutes, until the bacon is caramelized and crispy. Remove the pan from the oven and let the bacon rest for 5 minutes to cool. Store in an airtight container in the refrigerator for up to 1 week.

CRISPY WONTONS

Used in Chinese Chicken Salad (page 56).

Makes 3 cups   Prep Time: 5 minutes   Cook Time: 6 minutes

INGREDIENTS

2 cups neutral oil

10 wonton wrappers, cut into ½-inch strips

Kosher salt

INSTRUCTIONS

1. In a large pot, heat the oil over medium-high heat to 350°F. Line a tray or plate with paper towels.
2. Working in batches, sprinkle the sliced wonton wrappers into the hot oil, covering the surface. Rotate the wontons frequently to ensure they crisp evenly and turn a nice golden brown color, 2 to 3 minutes.
3. Remove the strips with a slotted spoon or spider strainer and place them on the prepared tray and sprinkle with salt. Repeat the process with the remaining wonton strips. Store in an airtight container at room temperature for up to 4 days.

CRISPY PROSCIUTTO

Used in Turkey Breakfast Club (page 48) and Emmanuel Duverneau's Caprese Chicken (page 69).

Makes 6 slices   Prep Time: 2 minutes   Cook Time: 12 minutes

INGREDIENTS

8 thin slices prosciutto

INSTRUCTIONS

1. Preheat the oven to 400°F. Line a sheet tray with parchment paper. Arrange the prosciutto slices on the sheet, leaving space between them.
2. Bake for 9 to 12 minutes, until the pieces begin to shrivel and start to get crispy. Remove from the oven and let cool for about 5 minutes; they will continue to crisp as they cool. Store in an airtight container in the refrigerator for up to 4 days.

SPICED NUTS

Used in Grilled Eggplant Caponata (page 135).

Makes ⅓ cup   Prep Time: 2 minutes   Cook Time: 5 minutes

INGREDIENTS

⅓ cup (1½ ounces) pine nuts or any of your favorite type of nut

½ teaspoon olive oil

2 pinches of kosher salt

Pinch of cayenne pepper

2 pinches of garlic powder

2 pinches of granulated sugar

INSTRUCTIONS

1. Preheat the oven to 350°F. Line a sheet tray with parchment paper. In a small bowl, toss the pine nuts with the olive oil, salt, cayenne, garlic powder, and sugar until well coated.
2. Spread the nuts on the prepared sheet tray and toast in the oven for about 5 minutes, until lightly toasted. Remove from the oven and cool. Store in an airtight container at room temperature for up to 1 week.

CRISPY ONIONS

Used in Albert Niazhvinski's Wellington Sando (page 126).

Makes 2 cups   Prep Time: 20 minutes   Cook Time: 5 minutes

INGREDIENTS

1 quart neutral oil

1 yellow onion sliced into ⅛-inch rings

1 cup buttermilk

1 cup all-purpose flour

1 tablespoon kosher salt

¼ teaspoon ground black pepper

1 teaspoon paprika

INSTRUCTIONS

1. In a countertop fryer or large pot, heat the oil over medium-high heat to 375°F. Line a plate with paper towels.
2. In a small bowl, separate the sliced onion rings and soak in the buttermilk for 15 minutes. In a medium bowl, combine the flour, salt, pepper, and paprika. Dredge the soaked onions individually in the flour mixture until well coated.
3. Working in small batches, place coated onions in the hot oil, flipping them with tongs or a slotted spoon, until golden brown, about 2 minutes. Remove the onions from the oil with a slotted spoon and drain on the prepared plate. Repeat until all the onion slices are fried. Use immediately or store in an airtight container.

PARM FRICO

Used in Nik Barricelli's Sicilian Steak Sandwich (page 85).

Makes 10 to 12 crisps   Prep Time: 5 minutes   Cook Time: 5 minutes

Be sure to use freshly shredded or a good quality pre-shredded Parmesan—the lower quality stuff cooks unevenly because of all the de-clumping additives.

INGREDIENTS

- 1 cup freshly shredded Parmesan cheese
- 1 teaspoon fresh oregano leaves, chopped
- 1½ teaspoons chopped fresh parsley leaves or parsley flakes

INSTRUCTIONS

1. Set an oven rack to the lowest level and preheat the oven to 375°F. Line a sheet tray with parchment paper.
2. Spread the cheese over the prepared tray in a thin, even layer. Sprinkle with the oregano and parsley. Bake for about 5 minutes, until light golden brown.
3. Remove from the oven (the frico will continue to crisp as they cool). Break apart into desired pieces. Store in an airtight container at room temperature for up to 4 days.

CRISPY GARLIC

Used in Spanish Prawns (page 70).

Makes ½ cup   Prep Time: 10 minutes   Cook Time: 10 minutes

INGREDIENTS

2 cups whole milk

10 garlic cloves, thinly sliced on a mandoline

2 cups neutral oil, for frying

Kosher salt

INSTRUCTIONS

Blanch the Garlic (First Round):

1. Heat 1 cup of the milk in a small saucepan over medium heat until it reaches the scalding point, just below boiling. Add the sliced garlic and stir gently. Let it blanch for 5 minutes. Strain the garlic, discarding the milk.

Blanch the Garlic (Second Round):

2. Repeat the process with the remaining 1 cup milk: scald, blanch the garlic for 5 minutes, then strain. Spread the garlic slices on paper towels and gently dab to remove excess moisture. This ensures the garlic fries evenly.

Fry the Garlic:

3. Heat the oil in a small saucepan to 325°F. Fry the garlic slices in small batches for about 3 minutes, flipping frequently to cook evenly.

4. Using a spider or slotted spoon, remove the garlic when it turns a light amber in color. Place on paper towels to drain excess oil. Sprinkle lightly with salt while still warm. Store in an airtight container at room temperature for up to 4 days.

ZESTY & PICKLED

Thai Pickles 212

Pickled Red Onion 213

Pickled Apricot 213

Giardiniera 214

Red Wine Cabbage 215

Corn Relish 215

THAI PICKLES

Used in Zach King's Steak Bánh Mì (page 91).

Makes 1 cup   Prep Time: 20 minutes

INGREDIENTS

¼ cup rice vinegar

2 tablespoons brown sugar

1 tablespoon kosher salt

1-inch piece fresh ginger, peeled and thinly sliced

Zest and juice of 1 lime

¼ cup julienned carrots (use a mandoline or cut into matchsticks)

¼ cup julienned daikon radish (use a mandoline or cut into matchsticks)

½ cup cucumber matchsticks (2 Persian cucumbers or ½ English cucumber, seeds removed)

1 jalapeño chile, thinly sliced, seeds removed to tone down the heat if desired

INSTRUCTIONS

1. In a large bowl, combine the vinegar, brown sugar, salt, ginger, and lime zest and juice. Whisk the mixture until well combined. Add the carrots, radish, cucumber, and chile to the bowl and let marinate for at least 30 minutes. Store in an airtight container in the refrigerator for up to 2 weeks.

PICKLED RED ONION

Used in Achiote Pork (page 120), Matt Stonie's Mississippi Shrimp Slugburger (page 101), and Pastrami Salmon (page 103).

Makes 1½ cups   Prep Time: 5 minutes   Cook Time: 10 minutes

INGREDIENTS

- 1 cup water
- ½ cup white wine vinegar
- 2 tablespoons granulated sugar
- 1 tablespoon kosher salt
- 1 tablespoon black peppercorns
- 1 tablespoon coriander seeds
- 2 bay leaves
- 1 red onion, thinly sliced

INSTRUCTIONS

1. In a small saucepan, combine the water, vinegar, sugar, salt, peppercorns, coriander seeds, and bay leaves. Place over medium heat and bring to a simmer to completely dissolve the sugar.
2. Add the sliced onion to the pan and let the onions sit in the simmering pickling liquid for 1 minute. Remove the pan from the heat and set aside to cool. Store in an airtight container in the refrigerator for up to 1 week.

PICKLED APRICOT

Used in Curried Chickpea Salad (page 62).

Makes ½ cup   Prep Time: 2 minutes   Cook Time: 10 minutes

INGREDIENTS

- ½ cup apple cider vinegar
- ¼ cup water
- 2 tablespoons honey
- ¼ cup dried apricots

INSTRUCTIONS

1. In a small pot, combine the vinegar, water, and honey. Place over medium heat and bring the mixture to a simmer. Add the apricots to the pot and simmer for 5 minutes, or until they are rehydrated and tender. Remove the apricots from the liquid and let them cool before using. Store in an airtight container in the refrigerator for up to 2 weeks.

GIARDINIERA

Used in Italian Beef (page 147).

Makes 1 quart   Prep Time: 15 minutes   Pickling Time: 3 days

INGREDIENTS

For the Brine:

2 cups small cauliflower florets

1 cup diced celery

1 cup diced yellow onion

½ cup diced carrots

½ cup diced red bell pepper

2 tablespoons finely diced jalapeño chile, or substitute green bell pepper for a milder pickle

3 tablespoons kosher salt

3 to 4 cups cold water

For the Pickles:

3 large garlic cloves

½ cup green olives, pitted then chopped

1 tablespoon fresh oregano leaves, chopped

1 teaspoon red chile flakes

½ teaspoon ground black pepper

1 cup distilled white vinegar

2 cups extra-virgin olive oil

INSTRUCTIONS

1. In a large bowl, combine the cauliflower florets, celery, onion, carrots, bell peppers, and chile. Stir in the salt and add enough cold water to cover the vegetables and brine. Cover the bowl with plastic wrap and refrigerate for 12 to 24 hours. Once brined, drain the salt water and rinse the vegetables. Set aside.

2. In a medium bowl, combine the garlic, olives, oregano, red chile flakes, pepper, and vinegar. Gradually whisk in the olive oil and then pour the mixture over the vegetables. Toss the vegetables lightly to combine. Cover and refrigerate for at least 48 hours before using. Store in an airtight container in the refrigerator for up to 2 weeks.

RED WINE CABBAGE

Used in Pastrami Egg and Cheese (page 51).

Makes 2 cups   Prep Time: 10 minutes   Cook Time: 1½ hours

INGREDIENTS

2 tablespoons neutral oil

½ medium red cabbage, shredded (3 cups)

¾ cups red wine

½ cup red wine vinegar

1 tablespoon granulated sugar

½ teaspoon caraway seeds

½ tablespoon kosher salt

⅓ cup water

3 tablespoons unsalted butter

INSTRUCTIONS

1. In a large skillet, heat the oil over medium heat. Add the cabbage and cook for about 10 minutes, until wilted and softened.
2. Stir in the wine, vinegar, sugar, caraway seeds, salt, and water. Bring to a simmer, then lower the heat to medium-low, cover, and cook for 40 minutes or until the liquid has reduced by half.
3. Stir in the butter and cook for another 30 minutes. Remove from the heat and adjust the seasoning to taste. Store in an airtight container in the refrigerator for up to 5 days.

CORN RELISH

Used in Pork Belly (page 55).

Makes 1 cup   Prep Time: 10 minutes   Cook Time: 10 minutes

INGREDIENTS

1 cup fresh yellow corn kernels (from about 1 ear)

3 tablespoons diced red bell pepper

1 tablespoon red Fresno chiles or jalapeño chiles, thinly sliced, seeds removed for less heat

3 tablespoons thinly sliced scallions

¼ cup diced Vidalia or white onion

½ cup cider vinegar

2 tablespoons honey

¼ teaspoon kosher salt

½ teaspoon mustard seeds, or substitute whole grain mustard

INSTRUCTIONS

1. Place the corn, bell pepper, chiles, scallions, and onion in a medium bowl.
2. In a small saucepan, combine the vinegar, honey, salt, and mustard seeds. Place over medium heat and bring to a boil. Remove from the heat and pour the hot mixture over the corn mixture. Set aside to cool to room temperature. Store in an airtight container in the refrigerator for up to 2 weeks.

INDEX

Achiote Pork, 120–21
Aioli
   Basil, 69
   Blue Cheese, 153
Albert Can Cook, 126
Albert Niazhvinski's Wellington Sando, 126–27
Alfajores, Coconut, 176–77
Apples, Cinnamon, Grilled Cheese, 185
appliances, small, xxi
Apricot, Pickled, 62–63, 213
Artichoke Tapenade, 83–84
Arugula
   Avocado Green Goddess Dressing, 194
   Bacon Jam and Chile Egg Biscuit, 43–45
   Blackened Salmon, 117
   Braised Lamb and Feta, 113–15
   Nik Barricelli's Sicilian Steak Sandwich, 85–87
   Salad or Mix, 59–60, 135–37
      Everything Chopped on an Everything Bagel, 23
      Grilled Eggplant Caponata, 135–37
      Susi Vidal's Spicy Chicken Parm, 59–60
   Turkey Breakfast Club, 48
Avocado
   Achiote Pork, 120–21
   Green Goddess Dressing, 99, 194
   Onigirazu: A Japanese Sushi Sandwich, 93–94
   Smash, 120–21
   Toast, 159

Bacon
   back, 10
   Sam Scow's Favorite Version of Elvis Presley's Favorite Sandwich, 4–5
   Fried Green BLT Sliders, 73–74
   Full English Breakfast Sandwich, 9–10
   Hot Honey, 7, 206
   Jam, 43–45
   Korean Street Toast, 25
   Turkey Breakfast Club, 48

Bagel, xxii
   Everything Chopped on an Everything Bagel 23
   Whitefish Salad Sandwich, 19
Baguette, xxii
   Chinese Chicken Salad, 56–57
   Shakshuka Sandwich, 35
   Spanish Prawns, 70–71
   Steak and Chimichurri, 153
   Zach King's Steak Bánh Mì, 91
Banana
   Banana Bread Sandwich, 178–79
   Sam Scow's Favorite Version of Elvis Presley's Favorite Sandwich, 4–5
   PB&J Stuffed Toast, 173
   Sauce, Carmelized, and Walnut Caramel, 178–79
Bánh Mì, Zach King's Steak, 91
Barricelli, Nik, 85
Basil
   Aioli, 69
   Mayo, 48, 201
   Pesto, 199
      Pistachio Tomato, 85–87
Bates, Kathy, 73–74
Batter
   Beer, 99
   Herb, 14–15
   Tempura, 75–77
   Triple-Decker Monte Cristo, 183
BBQ Sauce, 199
   Brisket Sandwich, 141–42
   Pulled Pork Sliders, 132–34
Beans
   Chilaquiles Torta, 20–21
   Full English Breakfast, 9–10
Beef
   Braised, and Feta, 113
   Brisket Sandwich, 141–42
   Chuck Roast, 147–49
   Corned
      Hong Kong-Style Egg Sandwich, 32

Beef, (cont.)
    Sauerkraut and, 66–67
    Sky High Reuben, 66–67
  Ground
    Currywurst, 131
    Kofta Pita, 118–19
  Italian, 147–49, 214
  Short Ribs, Braised, 108–9
  Steak
    Bánh Mì, 91, 212
    Carne Asada, 20–21
    Cheesesteak, 157–58
    Chimichurri and, 153, 195, 205
    Cowboy, 41–42
    Eggs and, 41–42
    Rib Eye and Red Wine Pan Sauce, 126–27
    Sicilian Sandwich, 85–87, 209
    Thai Marinated, 91
    Wellington Sando, 126–27
Beer-Battered Fish, No Chips, 99
Biscuits, xv, xxii
  Bacon Jam and Chile Egg, 43–45
  Buttermilk, 37–38, 43–45
  Fried Chicken 37–38
  store-bought, 45
Blackened Salmon, 117, 194
blenders, xxi
Blueberry
  Crème Fraîche, 186–87
  Lemon Curd Pound Cake Sandwich, 186–87
Bologna, 192
  and Cheese, Baby!, 65
breads
  deciding which is best, xvii
  storing, xxv
  toasting, xxvi
  types of, xxii-xxv
bread slicing machine, xiii
Brioche, xxii-xxiii, xxv
  Blackened Salmon, 117
  Espresso and, 189
  Fried Green BLT Sliders, 73–75
  Gruyère Toast, 16
  Herbaceous Crab Salad, 89
  Matt Stonie's Mississippi Shrimp Slugburger, 101
  PB&J Stuffed Toast, 173
  Thai Fried Chicken, 75–77
Brisket Sandwich, 141–42, 199
Broccoli Cheddar Melt, 125
burrito, 159
Butter, xvi, xxvi
  Garlic Herb, 79
Buttermilk
  Biscuits, 37–38, 43–45
  Chicken Marinade, 106
  Citrus Slaw, 132–34
  Pancake Griddle, 11–12
  Ranch Dressing, 117, 194

Cabbage
  Cauliflower Katsu, 123
  Chinese Chicken Salad, 56–57
  Korean Street Toast, 25
  Pineapple Jerk Chicken, 138–40
  Pulled Pork Sliders, 132–34
  Red Wine, 51, 215
  Slaw
    Buttermilk Citrus, 132–34
    Honey Mustard, 56–57
    Pineapple Jerk Chicken, 138–40
    Spicy Korean Chicken Sando, 106–7
Cajun Breakfast Sandwich, 3
Cajun Mayo, Spicy, 201
Cake, Pound, 186–87
Caponata, Grilled Eggplant, 135–37, 208
Caprese Chicken, Emmanuel Duverneau's, 69, 207
Caramelized
  Bananas, 4–5, 178–79
  Onions
    Currywurst, 131
    French-Style, 16–17, 145–46
Caramel Sauce
  Miso, 165
  Salted, 167
  Walnut and Caramelized Bananas, 178–79
Carne Asada
  Cheesesteak, 157–58
  Chilaquiles Torta, 20–21
Cauliflower
  Giardiniera, 214

Katsu, 123
challah, xxiii
    French Toast, 7
Cheese. *See also* Cream Cheese
    American
        Chopped Sausage Sandwich, 47
        Josh Scherer's Carne Asada Cheesesteak, 157–58
        Korean Street Toast, 25
        Pancake Griddle, 11–13
        Pork Roll, 31
    Blue Cheese Aioli, 153
    Brie, Triple-Decker Monte Cristo, 183
    Burrata, Grilled Eggplant Caponata, 135–37
    Cheddar
        Bologna and Cheese, Baby!, 65
        Broccoli Melt, 125
        Cajun Breakfast Sandwich, 3
        Cheesesteak, Josh Scherer's Carne Asada, 157–58
        Cinnamon Apple Grilled Cheese, 185
        Pimiento, 65
        Short Rib Toastie, 108–9
    Feta
        Braised Lamb and, 113
        Shakshuka Sandwich, 35
        Whipped, 198
    Goat
        Summer Squash Sandwich, 83–84
    Grilled
        Cinnamon Apple, 185
        Quintessential Grilled Cheese, 84
        tomato soup and, 109
    Gruyère
        Croque Monsieur, 151
        French Onion Omelet Sandwich, 16–17
        Short Rib Toastie, 108–9
        Toast, 16–17
    Mozzarella
        Emmanuel Duverneau's Caprese Chicken, 69
        Susi Vidal's Spicy Chicken Parm, 59–60
    Oaxaca or Monterey Jack
        Chilaquiles Torta, 20–21
    Parmesan
        Chicken, Susi Vidal's Spicy Chicken Parm, 59
        Parm Frico, 209
    Pepper Jack
        Chili Spiced French Toast Sandwich, 7
        Mumbai Masala Toast, 14–15
    Provolone
        Chicken French Dip, 145–46
        Chopped Sausage Sandwich, 47
        Italian Beef, 147–49
    Ricotta
        Green Eggs and Ham, 27
    Sauce
        Chipotle, 157–58
        Gruyère, 151
        three cheese, 125
    Swiss
        Pastrami Egg and 51
        Sky High Reuben, 66–67
        Tonkatsu Cubano, 129
Chermoula, 113–15, 153
Cherry
    Chocolate, on Sourdough, 191
    Compote, 191
Chicken
    Braised, and Jus, 145–46
    Caprese, 69
    Dredge, 37–38
    French Dip, 145–46
    Fried
        Biscuit, 37–38
        H Woo's Thai, 75–77
        Spicy Korean Sando, 106–7
    Marinade, 37–38, 106–7
    Parm, Susi Vidal's Spicy, 59–60
    Peri-Peri, 155, 157
    Pineapple Jerk, 138–40
    Rub, 155
    Salad, Chinese, 56–57, 207
    Spread, Five-Spice, 56–57
Chickpea
    Curried Salad, 62–63, 213
    Falafel Pita, 95–97
Chilaquiles Torta, xxviii, 20–21, 196
Chiles, xvi
    Carne Asada Cheesesteak, 157–58
    Chili Crisp, 205
    Chili Spiced French Toast Sandwich, 7
    Chipotle Cheese Sauce, 157–58

Chiles, (cont.)
    Chipotle Mayo, 132–34
    Coriander Chutney, 197
    Corn Relish, 215
    Egg Biscuit, and Bacon Jam, 43–45
    Fried Eggs, 43–45, 48
    Fig Jam, 183
    Giardiniera, 214
    Habanero Pickled Onions, 157–58
    Hot Honey, 55
    Hot Honey Bacon, 206
    Jerk Spice Blend Chicken Marinade, 138–40
    Papaya Salad, 75–77
    Red Zhoug Sauce, 118–19
    Salsa Verde, 196
    Spicy Ketchup, 203
    Spicy Tomato and Mushroom Chutney, 198
    Thai Fried Chicken, 75–77
    Thai Pickles, 212
    Triple-Decker Monte Cristo, 183
    Turkey Breakfast Club, 48
Chimichurri, 195
    Steak and, 153
Chinese Chicken Salad, 56–57
Chip Butty, 79
Chocolate
    Cherry on Sourdough, 191
    Ganache, 175
    Hazelnut Panini, 167
    Peanut Butter Whoopie Ice Cream Pie, 168–69
    Stroopwafel S'Mores, 175
Chorizo Tomato Sauce, 70–71
Chutney
    Coriander, 14, 197
    Spicy Tomato and Mushroom, 108, 198
ciabatta, xxiii
    Hazelnut Chocolate Panini, 167
    Steak and Eggs, 41–42
    Susi Vidal's Spicy Chicken Parm, 59–60
Cinnamon Apple Grilled Cheese, 185
Club Sandwich, Turkey Breakfast, 48
Coconut
    Alfajores, 176–77
    Cream Filling, 176–77
Compote
    Cherry, 191

    Cinnamon Apple, 185
    Strawberry, 173
    Sumac Strawberry, 181
Cookies
    Oatmeal, 171
    Shortbread, 176–77
    Stroopwafel S'Mores, 175
    Whoopie Pie, 158–59
Coriander Chutney, 14, 197
Corned Beef. See Beef, Corned
Corn Relish, 55, 215
Crab Salad
    Herbaceous Crab Salad Sandwich, 89
Cream
    Banana Bread Sandwich, 178–79
    Blueberry Crème Fraîche, 186–87
    Chantilly, 167, 178–79
    Yuzu, 163
    Espresso Whipped, 189
    Hazelnut Chocolate Panini, 167
    Oatmeal Peaches and Crème Pie, 171
Cream Cheese
    Dill and Lemon, 103
    Filling, 171
    Horseradish, 196
    Oatmeal Peaches and Crème Pie, 171
    Scallion, 23
    Sweet Mascarpone Spread, 191
Croissants, xxiii
    Cajun Breakfast Sandwich, 3–4
    Crispy, for Cinnamon Apple Grilled Cheese, 185
    Elvis Presley's Favorite Sandwich, 4
    Turkey Breakfast Club, 48
    Wellington Sando, 126–27
Croque Monsieur, 151
Cuban bread, xxiii
Cubano, Tonkatsu, 129
Cucumber
    Kofta Pita, 118–19
    Parsley Salad, 95–97
    Pickled, 141–42
    Raita, 62–63
    Thai Pickles, 212
    Tzatziki, 110–12
Curry
    Chickpea Salad, 62–63

Currywurst, 131
Ketchup, 203

Dijon Mayo, 202
Dill and Lemon Cream Cheese, 103
Donut Buns, 165
Dressing
    Avocado Green Goddess, 194
    Buttermilk Ranch, 194
    Thousand Island, 66–67
Duverneau, Emmanuel, 69

Eggplant Caponata, Grilled, 135–37
Eggs
    Bacon Jam and Chile Biscuit, 43–45
    baked, 39
    boiling, 7, 39, 81
    Cajun Breakfast Sandwich, 3
    Chilaquiles Torta, 20–21
    Chile Fried, 43–45, 48
    Chili Spiced French Toast Sandwich, 7
    Chopped Sausage Sandwich, 47
    Elvis Presley's Favorite Sandwich, 4–5
    fried, 39
    Full English Breakfast Sandwich, 9–10
    Garam Masala, 28–29
    Green, and Ham, xxviii, 27
    Hong Kong-Style, Sandwich, 32–33
    Korean Street Toast, 25
    Mumbai Masala Toast, 14–15
    Omelet, 39
        French Onion, Sandwich, 16–17
    Pancake Griddle, 11–13
    Pastrami, and Cheese, 51
    Poached, 35, 39
    Pork Roll, 31
    Salad, Japanese Style, 81
    scrambled, 39
        Hong Kong-Style, 32
        Pesto, 27
        Spiced, 28–29
    Shakshuka Sandwich, 35
    Steak and, 41–42
    Tonkatsu Cubano, 129
Emmanuel Duverneau's Caprese Chicken, 69
English Breakfast Sandwich, 9–10

English muffin bread, xxiii
equipment, xxi
Espresso
    Brioche and, 189
    Whipped Cream, 189
Everything Chopped on an Everything Bagel, 23

Falafel Pita, 95–97, 159
Feta
    Braised Lamb and, 113–15
    Shakshuka Sandwich, 35
    Whipped, 198
Fig Chile Jam, 183
Fish
    No Chips, 99
    Onigirazu: Japanese Sushi Sandwich, 93
    Salmon
        Blackened, 117
        Pastrami, 103
    Whitefish Salad Sandwich, 10
fish spatula, xxi
Five-Spice Chicken Spread, 56–57
Focaccia, xxiii
    Fresh, Sicilian Steak Sandwich, 85–87
food processors, xxi, 77
French Onion Omelet Sandwich, 16–17
French Toast, Chili Spiced Sandwich, 7
Fried Green Tomatoes (film), 73–74
Fruit Sando, 163
fryer, countertop, xxi

Ganache, 175
Garam Masala Eggs, 28–29
Garlic
    Crispy, 210
    Herb Butter, 79
    Sauce, 195
Giardiniera, 214
Ginger
    Chili Crisp, 205
    Pickled Tuna, 93–94
Gochujang, 25
    Honey Glaze, 106–7
    Spicy Ketchup, 203
Gravlax, Everything Chopped on and Everything
    Bagel, 23

Greek Turkey Meatball, 110–12
Green Eggs and Ham, xxviii, 27

Habanero Pickled Onions, 157–58
Ham
    Cajun Breakfast Sandwich, 3
    Green Eggs and, 27
    Hajji's Deli, 47
    Maple-Glazed, 27
    Pork Roll, 31
    Tasso, 3
    Taylor, 31
    Tonkatsu Cubano, 129
    Triple-Decker Monte Cristo, 183
hamburger, 159
Hazelnut Chocolate Panini, 167
Hellfire Club, 61
Herbs, xvi
    Avocado Green Goddess Dressing, 194
    Crab Salad, 89
    Chermoula, 113–15
    Chimichurri Sauce, 195
    Garlic Butter, 79
Hillel Sandwich, xii
hoagies, xxiii-xxiv
Honey
    Glaze, Gochujang, 106–7
    Hot, 55
    Hot Bacon, 206
    Peanut Butter Coating, 173
    Mustard Slaw, 56–57
Hong Kong-Style Egg Sandwich, 32–33
Horseradish Cream Cheese, 196
hot dog, 159
Hot Honey, 55
Hot Honey Bacon, 206
Hot Maple Syrup, 37–38
Hummus, Falafel Pita, 95–97
H Woo's Thai Fried Chicken, 75–77

Ice Cream
    Chocolate Peanut Butter Fudge, 171
    Chocolate Peanut Butter Whoopie Ice Cream
        Pie, 168–69
    Miso Sesame, 165
Italian Beef, 147–49

Jam
    Bacon, and Chili Egg Biscuit, 43
    Chile Fig, 183
    Peri-Peri, 156
Japanese Egg Salad, 81
Japanese Sushi Sandwich, Onigirazu, 93–94
Jerk Chicken, Pineapple, 138–40
Jerk Spice Blend, 138–40
Josh Scherer's Carne Asada Cheesesteak, 157–58

Katsu, Cauliflower, 123
Ketchup
    Curry, 203
    Spicy, 203
Kimchi
    Mayo, 106–7
    Tonkatsu Cubano, 129
King, Zach, 91
knives, xxi
Kofta Pita, 118–19
Korean Chicken Sando, Spicy, 106–7
Korean Street Toast, 25
kosher deli, first, xiii

Labneh,
    Sumac Strawberry and Sweet Labneh, 181
Lamb
    Braised, and Feta, 113–15
    Kofta Pita, 118–19
Lee, H Woo, 75
Lee, Mrs. N.K.M., xiii
Lemon
    Curd and Blueberry Pound Cake Sandwich, 186–87
    Dill and, Cream Cheese, 103

mandolin, xxi
Manganaro's food emporium, 47
Maple
    Glazed Ham, 27
    Mustard, Spicy, 11–13
    Pancakes, Griddle, 11–13
    Syrup, Hot, 37–38
Marinade
    Achiote Pork, 120–21

Chicken, 37–38
    Jerk Spice, 138–40
        Spicy Korean Chicken Sando, 106–7
Maru Los Angeles, 75
Mascarpone Spread, Sweet, 191
mason jars, xxi
Matt Stonie's Mississippi Shrimp Slugburger, 101
Mayo, xxvi
    Basil, 201
    Basil Aioli, 69
    Blue Cheese Aioli, 153
    Chipotle, 132–34
    Dijon, 202
    Kimchi, 106–7
    Spicy Cajun, 201
    Spicy Remoulade, 73–74
    Spicy Thai, 91
    Whole Grain Mustard, 202
McGriddle, 11–13
Meatball, Greek Turkey, 110–12
microplane, xxi
milk bread, xxv, xvii, 33
Mint Yogurt, 28–29
mise en place, xv
Miso
    Caramel Sauce, 165
    Mustard, 129
    Sesame, 165
Monte Cristo, Triple-Decker, 183
mortar and pestle, 77
Mumbai Masala Toast, 14–15
Mushrooms
    Albert Niazhvinski's Wellington Sando, 126–27
    Chutney, Spicy Tomato and, 198
    Full English Breakfast, 9–10
Mustard
    Dijon Mayo, 202
    Honey Slaw, 56–57
    Miso, 129
    Spicy Maple, 11–13
    Whole Grain, Mayo, 202
Mythical Kitchen, 157

Naan, xxv
Nathan's Hot Dog Eating Competition, 101
Niazhvinski, Albert, 126

Nik Barricelli's Sicilian Steak Sandwich, 85–87
Nuts
    Hazelnut Chocolate Panini, 167
    Spiced, 208

Oatmeal Peaches and Crème Pie, 171
oils, xvi
Omelet, 39
    French Onion, Sandwich, 16–17
    Hong Kong-Style Egg Sandwich, 32
    Korean Street Toast, 25
Onigirazu, 93–94
Onions
    Brisket Sandwich, 145–46
    Caramelized, 131
        Currywurst, 131
        French-Style, 145–46
    Crispy, 208
    Golden, 28–29
    French, Omelet Sandwich, 16–17
    Kofta Pita, 118–19
    Pickled
        Giardiniera, 214
        Habanero, 157–58
        Red, 213
    Roasted Red, 117
    Sumac, 113–15, 118–19
Orange, Mandarin, Fruit Sando, 163

Pancake Griddle Sandwich, xxviii, 11–13
panini press, xxi
pantry items, xvi-xix
Papaya Salad, 75–77
parchment paper, xxi
Parmesan
    Parm Frico, 209
    Chicken, 59–60
Pastrami
    Egg and Cheese, 51
    Salmon Sandwich, 103
PB&J Stuffed Toast, 173
Peaches, Oatmeal, and Crème Pie, 171
Peanut Butter
    Chocolate Whoopie Ice Cream Pie, 168–69
    PB&J Stuffed Toast, 173

Peppers, Bell
   Corn Relish, 215
   Giardiniera, 214
   Italian Beef, 147–49
   Kofta Pita, 118–19
   Red, Pistou, 135–37, 147–49
   Red Zhoug Sauce, 118–19
   Shakshuka Sandwich, 35
   Tomato Sauce, 35
Peri-Peri Chicken, 155
Pesto, 199
   Green Eggs and Ham, 27
   Pistachio Tomato, 85–87
   Scrambled Eggs, 27
Pickles / Pickled
   Apricot, 213
   Cucumbers, 141–42
   Giardiniera, 214
   Onions
      Habanero, 157–58
      Red, 213
   Thai, 212
Pimiento Cheese, 65
Pineapple Jerk Chicken, 138–40
Pistachio Tomato Pesto, 85–87
pita, xxv, xvii
   Falafel, 95–97, 159
   Kofta, 118–19
pizza rolls, 159
pop tart, 159
Pork. *See also* Ham
   Achiote Pork, 120–21
   Pork Belly, 55
   Pulled, Sliders, 132–34
   Roll, 31
   Tonkatsu Cubano, 129
Potatoes
   Bologna and Cheese, Baby!, 65
   Chip Butty, 79
   Crispy Shoestring, 205
   Chips, Homemade, 64–65
   frozen, 79
   Mumbai Masala Toast, 14–15
   Spiced Mashed, 14–15
pots and pans, xxi

Pound Cake, 186–87
Presley, Elvis, 4
pretzel bread, xxv
Prosciutto
   Crispy, 207
   Wellington Sando, 126–27

quesadilla, 159
Quintessential Grilled Cheese, 84

Raita, 62–63
Ramsay, Gordon, viii-xi
Ranch Dressing, Buttermilk, 194
Red Pepper Pistou, 135–37, 147–49
Red Zhoug Sauce, 118–19
Relish, Corn, 215
Remoulade, Spicy, 73–74
Reuben Sandwich, 52
   Sky High, xxvi, 66–67
Rohwedder, Otto, xiii
Rice, Sticky, 93–94
Ricotta, Green Eggs and Ham, 27
ring cutter, xxi
rye bread, xxv

Salsa Verde, 196
Salted Caramel Sauce, 167
Sam Scow's Favorite Version of Elvis Presley's
   Favorite Sandwich, 4–5
Sandwich, John Montagu, 4th Earl of, 61
sandwiches
  anatomy, xiv
  defined, 159
  history of, xii-xiv
  most expensive, 84
  number eaten per day, xiii
  world's largest, 67
Sauce
  BBQ, 132, 141, 199
  Caramel
    Miso, 165
    Salted, 167
    Walnut, 178–79
  Chermoula, 113–15
  Chimichurri, 195

Cheese
    Chipotle, 157–58
    Gruyère, 151
Garlic, 195
Gochujang Honey Glaze, 106–7
Red Pepper Pistou, 135–37
Red Wine Pan, 126–27
Red Zhoug, 118–19
Salsa Verde, 196
Tomato
    Chorizo, 70–71
    Greek, 110–12
    Pepper, 35
Tonkatsu, 123, 129
Sauerkraut, Corned Beef and, 66–67
Sausage
    Chopped Sandwich, 47
    Chorizo Tomato Sauce, 70–71
    Currywurst, 131
    Pancake Griddle, 11–13
    Patties, 131
    Spanish Prawns, 70–71
Scallion Cream Cheese, 23
Scherer, Josh, 157
Scow, Sam, 4
Serendipity 3 restaurant, 84
Sesame
    Ice Cream, Black, 165
    Miso, 165
Seuss, Dr., xxviii
Shakshuka Sandwich, 35
Shepard, Alan, 41
Shortbread Cookies, 176–77
Short Rib Toastie, 108–9
Shrimp
    Mississippi Slugburger, 101
    Patties, 101
    Spanish Prawns, 70–71
Sicilian Steak Sandwich, Nik Barricelli's, 85–87
Sky High Reuben, xxvi, 66–67
Slaw
    Buttermilk Citrus, 132–34
    Honey Mustard, 56–57
    Pineapple Jerk Chicken, 138–40
    Spicy Korean Chicken Sando, 106–7

Sliders
    Fried Green BLT, 73–74
    Pulled Pork, 132–34
S'Mores, Stroopwafel, 175
sourdough bread, xxv
Spanish Prawns, 70–71
spices, xvi
Spicy / Spiced, xvi-xvii
    Cajun Mayo, 201
    Ketchup, 203
    Korean Chicken Sando, 104, 106–7
    Maple Mustard, 11–13
    Mashed Potatoes, 14–15
    Nuts, 208
    Remoulade, 73–74
    Rub, for Italian Beef, 147–49
    Thai Mayo, 91
    Tomato and Mushroom Chutney, 198
spider, xxi
Spinach
    Bacon Jam and Chile Egg Biscuit, 43–45
    Garam Masala Eggs, 28–29
    Green Eggs and Ham, 27
sprouted wheat bread, xxv
Squash, Summer, Sandwich, 83–84
stand mixer, xx
stocks and broths, xvii
Stonie, Matt, 101
Strawberries
    Compote, 173
    Fruit Sando, 163
    PB&J Stuffed Toast, 173
    Sumac, and Sweet Labneh, 181
Stroopwafel S'Mores, 175
subs
    first six-foot, 47
    named, 87
Sumac
    Kofta Pita, 118–19
    Onions, 113–15, 118–19
    Strawberry Compote, 181
Sushi Sandwich, Japanese, Onigirazu, 93–94
Susi Vidal's Spicy Chicken Parm, 59–60

taco, 159
Tandy, Jessica, 73–74
Tapenade, Archichoke, 83–84
Tempura Batter, 75–77
Thai Fried chicken, H Woo's, 75–77
Thai Pickles, 212
Thai Steak Bánh Mì, Zach King's, 91
thermometers, xxi
Thousand Island Dressing, 66–67
Toast, xxvi
   Korean Street, 25
   Mumbai Masala, 14–15
   PB&J Stuffed, 173
Tomatillos, Salsa Verde, 196
Tomatoes
   Blistered Cherry, 59–60
   Chutney, Spicy Mushroom and, 198
   Fried Green, BLT Sliders, 73–74
   Jam, Peri-Peri, 155
   Pesto, Pistachio, 85–87
   Roasted Smear, 9–10
   sun-dried, 59
   Sauce
      Chorizo, 70–71
      Greek, 110–12
      Pepper, 35
Tonkatsu
   Cubano, 129
   Sauce, 123
Triple-Decker Monte Cristo, 183
Tuna, Pickled Ginger, 93–94
Turkey
   Breakfast Club, 48
   Herb Butter, 48
   Meatball, Greek, 110–12
   Triple-Decker Monte Cristo, 183
Tzatziki, 110–12

Vegetables
   Egg Patty, 25
   Giardiniera, 214
Vidal, Susi, 59–60
vinegars, xvii

Walnut Caramel Sauce, 178–79
Wellington Sando, Abert Niazhvinski's, 126–27
Whitefish Salad Sandwich, 10
Whole Grain Mustard Mayo, 202
Whoopie Pie Cookies, Chocolate Peanut Butter Cream Pie, 171
Wine, Red
   Cabbage, 215
   Pan Sauce, 126–27
Wonder Bread, xiii
Wontons, Crispy, 207

Yogurt
   Mint, 28–29
   Raita, 62–63
   Tzatziki, 110–12
Yuzu Chantilly Cream, 163

Zach King's Steak Bánh Mì, 91
zip-top bags, xxi

ABOUT THE TEAM

IDIOT SANDWICH

Idiot Sandwich started as a viral comedy sketch featuring Gordon Ramsay, garnering millions of views across YouTube and TikTok before eventually becoming a popular meme. The digital-first content series born from this piece of internet culture launched in 2024 and features some of YouTube and TikTok's biggest creator talent—from Zach King and Albert Can Cook to Rhett McLaughlin and Link Neal. Each episode sees talent competing to create an epic sandwich that will see them crowned the ultimate Idiot Sandwich by Gordon Ramsay himself.

GORDON RAMSAY

Internationally renowned, multi-Michelin-starred chef Gordon Ramsay has over ninety restaurants globally. He's also renowned for highly successful and award-winning original programming. Emmy-nominated and BAFTA-winning, he produces TV shows on both sides of the Atlantic, seen by audiences worldwide in more than two hundred territories. He is the only talent on air in the US with five prime-time national network shows, as well as being the face of Bite, a new digital food platform that was launched in partnership with FOX Entertainment in 2023. Gordon has over one hundred million followers across social, has published over twenty-five books, and has sold over ten million copies worldwide in total.

COURTNEY McBROOM

Courtney McBroom is a chef, culinary producer, and the author of this book. She's written lots of other great books, too, including *Party People, Divine Your Dinner, All About Cake, Momofuku Milk Bar,* and *Milk Bar Life.* She is the founder of *Ruined Table*, a publishing and event series about dinner parties, and was the head food consultant for *Lessons in Chemistry* on Apple TV+. She has been a guest on shows including *Chef's Table, Mind of a Chef, Vice Munchies,* and *Bong Appétit,* and her writing and recipes have been featured in *Food & Wine, Vice, GQ, InStyle, Thrillist, Stylist,* and *Lucky Peach* magazine. She loves a good party, and she humbly believes that hot dogs are, in fact, sandwiches.

BITE BOOKS

Bite is all about great food, great stories, and making cooking exciting for everyone. Created by FOX Entertainment in partnership with Gordon Ramsay and Harper Influence, it brings together America's favorite food television programs, the latest digital originals, and the most exciting food stars and creators. Now, with Bite Books, we're bringing that same energy to the kitchen with a new collection of cookbooks designed for home cooks of all levels. From expert tips to easy, delicious recipes, Bite Books is made to inspire and entertain. Bite Books is a division of Studio Ramsay Global.

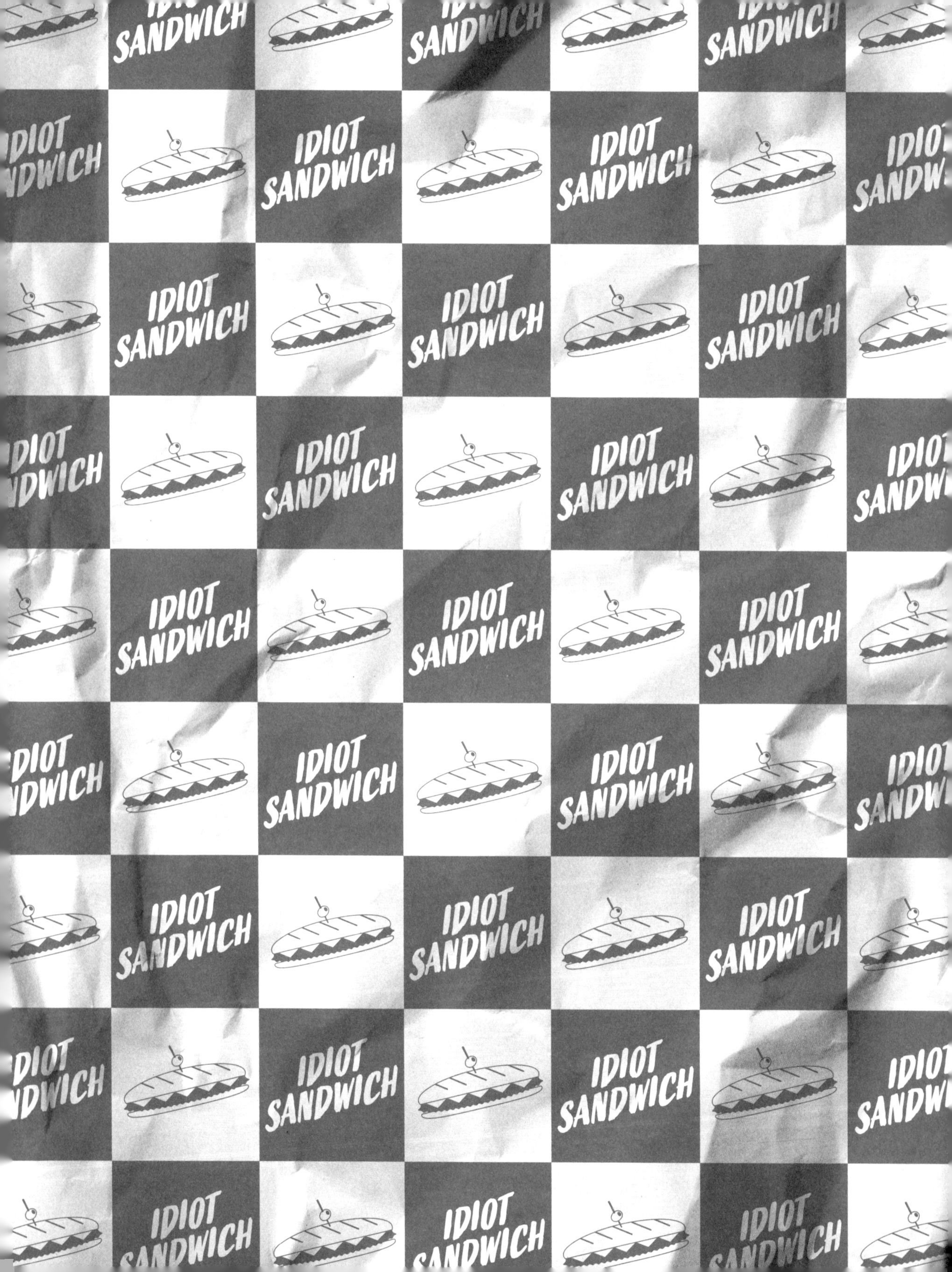
IDIOT SANDWICH